Diary of a Gay, Pregnant Bride

A memoir

by

Kelly Frankenberg

This is a work of nonfiction. Names in this memoir have been changed to protect the innocent…and the guilty.

For my parents, especially my mother, whom I may never fully understand but love with all my heart.

Acknowledgements

Thanks to my parents, especially my mother, for making me the person I am today. Thanks to all my teachers, professors, friends, and relatives who supported me and inspired me. Thanks to those who helped me with my grammar issues and my writing, especially Luanne Frankenberg, Amber Bathke, Leah Phifer, Gail Gifford, Emily Spence, and Laura Vaillancourt. Thanks especially to Kristen Iversen for all her guidance and wisdom, and Jean Berry for her intuitive support. Thanks to the former mayor of Minneapolis, R.T. Rybak for legally marrying us and all his support. Extra special thanks to Donna and Todd.

Table of Contents

"When one door of happiness closes, another opens; but often we look so long at the closed door that we do not see the one which has been opened for us."

– Helen Keller

It was this moment that not only would be stamped in my memory, as every first time bride, but would also be a documented part of history, the snapshot heading straight to the Minnesota Historical Society. It was this moment I pledged my love to the woman I was marrying for the second time, first time legally, and first time in front of television station cameras, newspaper reporters, and the mayor of Minneapolis. Donna, my partner, our son, Todd, our two witnesses, and I stood with Mayor R.T. Rybak on the steps of City Hall, catching the flashes of cameras in our eyes like a red carpet event. One hand held Donna's and one hand held my pregnant belly of seven months. Feeling like a celebrity, I looked out into the crowd that filled the atrium and the other gay couples waiting for their chance to become legal. It was 2:14 a.m. on August 1, 2013.

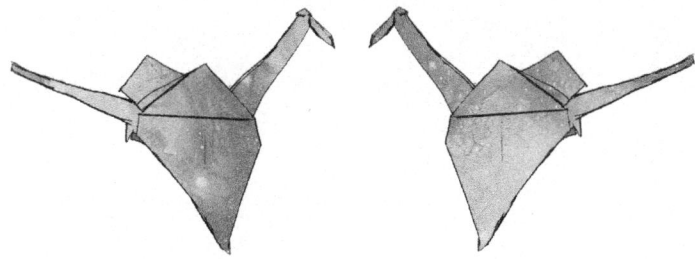

Diary of a Gay, Pregnant Bride

PART ONE:
THE PLANS

<u>April 2012</u>

"It's okay to cry, honey," Mom said.

I stood in my mother's living room because I didn't want to sit. The chairs looked uncomfortable and unwelcoming. The forest green hue of the easy chairs matched the pine trees that flooded the large window. I stared out the window because I couldn't look at my mother.

Disappointment joined my anger and sadness. I thought it would work out like it usually did. Why were all my plans falling apart? I just wanted to get married.

Planning a wedding shows you a lot about yourself. You may focus on aspects you hadn't thought were important to you before. You may find yourself holding on to some ridiculous tradition when you don't even like it.

For me, planning my wedding only confirmed I'm more anal and controlling like my mother than I thought; however, those two qualities do produce a decent final product. It seemed my mother's product was me. My product was the wedding.

As almost every young girl dreams about her wedding, I did, too. I planned for a big Catholic church filled with people and for a white dress that I designed and my mother sewed, with silver sequins and cut-out butterflies. I pictured the bridesmaids' dresses each a color of the rainbow and the guys with matching ties. The flower girl wearing purple butterfly wings like a fairy. A perfect wedding cake my mother decorated. My father walking me down the aisle and giving me away to my handsome Italian groom. Sun coming in the church's stained glass windows and God nodding with approval. All my relatives and friends sharing in the happiest day of my life.

As this pivotal day approached, however, I had to let go of every wedding fantasy I ever manifested. We won't be getting married in a Catholic church or any church. My fiancée isn't Catholic, but now, neither am I. Our marriage won't be legal in our state of Minnesota because we are both women. My father can't walk me down the aisle because he is no longer living. My mother can't sew the dress I designed or decorate my cake because she is too sick from chemo treatments.

Forced to improvise, my partner, Donna, and I decided to have a destination wedding in Hawaii, just us and "Momtom" (my mother and my stepdad, Tom). Donna's parents were quite elderly and sickly to travel.

Yet as I stood in my mother's living room that day, my adult dreams of a Hawaiian wedding were crushed, also.

"I'm just too sick to go, honey. I can't see myself getting on another airplane for a really long time. I don't have any energy left."

I looked at her for the first time since I entered the living room. I saw the sadness on her face from my disappointment. Her light aqua eyes looked gray and tired. She lay on the pastel pink chaise lounge under a matching blanket her father made. It was in this wretched living room that Mom told me her cancer had come back. It was in this living room that my father told me he had only months left to live. I should have called it the dying room.

While ignoring the idea of losing another parent, I tried to accept losing another wedding fantasy. Donna and I would still go to Hawaii for our honeymoon, but now there were fewer than four weeks to get married before we left.

"Can we have the wedding in your backyard?" I asked Mom. Her eyes, which now lacked eyelashes, were closed, resting. She slowly opened them without moving her head or the white hat which covered her mostly bald scalp.

"Sure, that would be nice," she said.

Being my mother's only child, a three-pound preemie born a week before Christmas, I always felt too special. But today I felt the sense of abandonment. Déjà vu. I had felt that before. The first time my mother had cancer she thought she wouldn't make it to my college graduation ceremony. The feeling of being your only family member at an important life event is like wearing an orphan's shoes. The kind you picture from movies: too big or too small, dusty, worn, and more holes than a pair of socks.

Despite her cancer, my mother did come to my graduation from art college that May of 2003. But I still needed her at one of the last major events in my life.

Since the honeymoon was scheduled for the middle of May, Donna and I decided to get married on May 6, a day that worked for most of our close friends. But now that meant I only had three weeks to plan a ceremony, pull it off, and get ready for the reception for over 200 family members and friends in June.

I wrote my list:

Ceremony
Invitations
Dress
Video
Food
Shoes
Photos
Hair
Flowers
Candle
Cake
Music
Rings

Ceremony

As I pictured the ceremony in my mother's backyard, I tried to romanticize the atmosphere: the willow tree my dad planted blowing in a subtle wind, birds singing, purple and pink flowers in pots, saying our vows under the white trellis. However, negative thoughts painted over grandeur. I saw my white shoes and dress ruined with grass stains, ticks crawling up the legs of the wedding party and guests, and deer flies landing on people's heads. And worst of all, I saw snakes crawling through the lawn from Momtom's recent snake infestation.

I forced myself to put aside these thoughts and focus on what needed to be done. First, I had to pay $800 to cancel the officiant in Hawaii, and then find a local officiant who was available on the day we chose.

When I found someone online who could perform a commitment ceremony for a good price, I chose the wordings myself to make it not too church-like. Donna wasn't comfortable with anything religious, but I also wanted to represent my spiritual background. As I e-mailed words back and forth with the officiant, she told me legally they were not allowed to say the word "marriage" at the ceremony. I accepted that our state did not recognize our marriage and that it would not be legal, but I hadn't anticipated not even being able to say the word "marriage." For the first time I really felt the discrimination and unfairness towards my marriage to Donna. I didn't mind calling it a union or a commitment, but I didn't like being told what I couldn't call it.

When I first told my mom I wanted to marry Donna, she was going through a period accepting she could be dying.

"Mom, I want to marry Donna. We want to live together."

"You really know that this is what you want?"

"Yes. I'm sure. Didn't you say you knew right away with Dad? That when you know you know."

"Yes."

"And I know she has a son. I love kids. I want a family."

"You can't even legally get married in Minnesota, right?"

"No," I said looking down.

Donna and I couldn't get a mortgage from Fannie Mae or Freddy Mac because they didn't recognize us together unless we were legally married. Partly since Mom felt she was dying, she helped us get a mortgage and appliances we needed.

"I only want to make sure you still have a relationship with God. And that you still have your faith," Mom said to me. Her eyebrows lost expression as the brown dust from the eyebrow pencil faded away, the only make-up she wore now.

Donna's family was Buddhist but they didn't practice it. Growing up in Vietnam she didn't know much about God at all. The only experience she had with religion or Christianity was her husband getting so far into it that viewpoints divided them.

My spiritual experience had been like a fishing lure. I'd dive into the lake of faith and then be yanked back up out of it again. I dove into faith first with the Catholic church, then the Lutheran church, then Assembly of God, non-denominational, finding God in nature, studying Islam, Buddhism, Christ Church of the Big Bang, to finally being spiritual. Faith was still with me though I didn't feel religious.

Knowing Donna didn't know much about God or that she wasn't raised under a religion, I noticed her spirit wasn't any different from anyone else's. She loved, cared, and had good moral values and a positive outlook on life and how people should live. Donna didn't need religion to tell her how to be kind or live her life.

My friend, Becky, once told me that God was an elephant and religion was blind men standing around it, each holding a part. One says, "I know what God is. God is this trunk." Another says, "No. I know what God is. God is this tail." Another says, "No. God is this foot." All of them are right but they are all missing the larger picture no one can see.

I kept my faith in God except it was no longer through any religion. I felt that faith was knowing that life is more than just a bunch of beautiful coincidences.

Invitations

I tried to have faith that my mother would be able to come to my wedding ceremony. As I wrote out invitations I thought if my mother felt better she would have liked to help; she was great at crafts. Yet I sat amongst the five empty chairs at the kitchen table Donna and I bought. The marble swirls of black and white on the hard surface felt cold and smooth. I didn't have any sisters or good friends who lived close to help me. Being an only child and as controlling and meticulous and creative as I was, I wanted to do it all myself anyway. And being an artist going back to school for writing, I didn't have much else to do while Donna was at work.

I didn't know what to call a gay wedding. Since I couldn't legally even say the word "marriage" at the ceremony, should I say it on the invitations? If I said a party or celebration, that made it less official.

I also had to consider whom to invite. I asked my uncle if I should invite my great aunt, Doreen. Aunt Doreen was very Christian and used to work for Billy Graham. She believed everything in the Bible as it was written. She once lived in Loring Park, one of the neighborhoods with the highest gay population in our state. She would say, "The gays are out again," in a frustrated voice when we'd pick her up to go somewhere. She would be shocked to know the gays were closer than she thought.

"You should invite Doreen," my uncle said. "At least give her the choice to make for herself."

After I sent the invitations I called my uncle again. Uncle Lou was my dad's last living brother and he very much resembled Dad.

"So Doreen called me the other day," he said.

"What did she say?"

"She asked me if I was coming to your wedding and I said ya. Then I asked if she was going and she said she didn't think she could bring herself to go."

"Oh, really?"

"So I asked her, I said, 'So Doreen, do you think I'm a good person?' And she said, 'Well, yes.' And I said, 'But because I don't believe in Jesus I'm going to hell?' And she said, 'Well, yes.' Then she told me to read the Bible and keep an open mind. I just laughed."

"Ya, a mind as open as hers, huh?"

"So I told her that it's so hard to find love in this world and if someone finds it you should be happy for them. I think she's starting to change; she said she should be more open. But don't be surprised if she doesn't come."

"Sorry you had to deal with her on that subject, but thanks," I said.

"Oh, it's no problem for me," he said. I pictured his face. His cheekbones stuck out like my dad's and his thinning white hair didn't cover all of his head, yet somehow he still looked close to handsome. His blue eyes hid behind his glasses. My green eyes didn't resemble my parents' blue, but I liked being different.

I folded paper cranes and glued them to the front of the invitations. I told Donna I wanted to represent her culture and background by adding an Asian theme to the wedding. When she saw my origami she said, "You know I'm not Japanese, right?" Her Vietnamese accent sounded sarcastic and sweet. She smiled.

Donna let me take care of almost all the wedding details. She wanted it to be simple, since she had been married before and was tired of over-the-top Vietnamese traditional weddings. Letting me take care of the details also caused fewer disagreements.

I looked down at the invitations. The white of the cranes contrasted with the purple of the paper. The cranes I folded for name markers sat on the kitchen table. I noticed one's wing hanging lower, forcing it to fall over. Picking it up to fix it, I read the name. Brenda. It was my mother's. Her broken wing of health and happiness weighted her down and wouldn't let her back up. I was able to fix it, but it was only paper.

The next week I received a card in the mail from Aunt Doreen. It read:

Dear Kelly,

I had prayed that the Lord would give you a loving Christian husband. It appears that that prayer isn't going to be answered in the way I had thought. The main thing is that you know The Lord Jesus as your personal Savior and

Lord. Then all else of life falls into its proper place. The picture of you and Donna is beautiful. I look forward to meeting her–

Love, Aunt Doreen

If an 80-year-old woman can see through new eyes, perhaps there is hope for the rest of the world.

Dress

The next day I drove to see the wedding dress I found online. I remembered my dream I had the night before. I dreamed I was shopping for a silver wedding dress and the sales lady helping me said if it wasn't white then people would think I wasn't a virgin. Then I found out she was a prostitute.

My mother had come into this world as the first child to a twenty-year old couple who proceeded to have six more. There are three boys and four girls. Each of my mother's sisters has a personality trait of my mother. There's the giggly one, the quiet one, and the stubborn one (Aunt Giggly, Aunt Quiet, and Aunt Stubborn; though I never call them those names in person).

As I drove the few hours north of Minneapolis I chatted with Mom's sister as she rode in the passenger seat of my electric blue Mini Cooper. Her cream-colored shih tzu, Tootsie, sat on her lap. This one was the quiet sister, so I did most of the talking.

"I wanted my wedding dress to be white with a little hint of color and something that sparkled," I told Aunt Quiet.

Originally I had drawn a design. Mom told me if I got a pattern she would help sew it.

Frankenberg, Kelly. <u>Dress Designs</u>. 2012.

Mom always sewed my clothes when I was little, working often in her sewing room on projects. When I learned to sew, I liked to design and make clothes; but I never used a pattern, so my outfit never fit right or hung right. This irritated Mom because she would have to try to fix it. I gave up on sewing and stuck with what I did best: design.

This time I bought a pattern for my dress, but after I showed it to Mom she said, "I wish you'd just find a dress you like. It would be easier. I don't think I'll feel well enough to help."

I ignored my disappointment. By now I was used to plans not going my way. The search for a dress already made would begin.

"After searching forever I finally found one I liked," I said, continuing the story. "But it was too short. I wrote down the name of the designer and looked online. I didn't think they made a long version, though it was worth a look."

My aunt sat quietly and listened, saying "oh ya" a few times in her stereotypical Minnesotan accent. The only blonde in the family, her hair bordered on platinum and hung to her shoulders with a few curls. She had a love for motorcycles and cute little dogs.

"I couldn't believe it when I found the long version. Unfortunately, it was $400 and no store would order it in for me to try unless I bought it first. I had to find a store that already had one. After calling 24 stores, I got lucky with the 25th, though three hours away."

Tootsie sat as silently as Aunt Quiet and enjoyed the ride.

"It was meant to be, just like my prom dress in high school."

"Oh, ya."

"I had found the perfect prom dress online and ordered it, but the website said it wasn't available till a month after my prom. So we cancelled the order and bought a different one at a store. But exactly a week before prom the dress I wanted magically arrived in the mail!"

I remembered my prom dress well; a long gold gown covered in black transparent fabric with black lace on the chest. Mom sewed some embroidered, colorful butterflies on the side to complete it.

Though this time, Mom was too sick to come with me to try on my dress. Mom had told me to call her sister because her sister had a broken foot and was off work. I didn't want a replacement for my mother, but I didn't want to go alone, either.

When my aunt and I arrived in the small Midwestern town of Little Falls, we left Tootsie in the car and my aunt hobbled to sit in a chair by the fitting room. Her black foot brace was wrapped tightly around her jeans.

I looked around the shop. Colorful prom dresses hung on white walls like paintings. Wedding gowns filled a row the length of the store. All were white. The white gowns looked so blank like a canvas waiting to be painted with the colorful joys of married life. A clearance rack separated the prom section from the wedding section. My dress was technically a prom dress and that thought added another less official wedding feeling. I avoided looking at the other daughters with their mothers browsing and trying on dresses as a store employee approached me.

"Hi. I called about a dress," I said.

"Yes, let me get it for ya," she said. Her enthusiasm made her Minnesota accent sound forced, or the other way around. Either way the enthusiasm wasn't contagious. I glanced at my aunt and then at the only mannequin inside the store. Oddly, the only mannequins wearing dresses were in the front window. This particular mannequin had no head. It reminded me of the mural boards I painted for events with cut-out heads that waited for a real person to put their face into in order to come alive.

The attendant came back with the dress. I put it on, four sizes too big, but I knew it was the perfect style. She then tied the back of the dress to give the illusion of a good fit. I could then order the dress in my size to be picked up at a shop closer to home.

"Wow, you look perfect," Aunt Quiet said.

"Thanks," I said, looking in the mirror. My hair was straight and thin. I changed the color every so often. The current color, reddish brown, fell in strands to the middle of my back. It made me look feminine even with barely any make-up on. The bead-work at the top of the dress sparkled in the shop's light. This was supposed to be an exciting and joyful moment. The absence of my mother only reminded me of what life would be like without her one day. I forced a smile for the mirror.

Donna and I had decided on black for our bridesmaids' color, since it was last minute. We figured our bridesmaids all owned a black dress or could borrow one. When my mother and I went dress shopping for my father's funeral I wanted any color except black; I couldn't stand wearing the depression on the outside. Now I could only hope the black bridesmaid dresses would look elegant and formal instead of depressing and funereal.

As a teenager, I had visualized a wedding in the colors of my painting palette, a full-color rainbow, not knowing the rainbow represented the gay community to which I would belong.

Video

It was easy to find a videographer on Craigslist more than happy to film a gay wedding. I thought about the last time I was in front of a camera for a long period of time. It was for an episode of Showtime's *The L Word,* filmed on a gay cruise, the gay cruise on which I came out of the closet.

<u>Fall 2004</u>

When I was 23 I explored my sexuality. I always felt more comfortable with women and I never had a huge desire on a sexual level, especially for men. My online friend, Becky, suggested we take a gay cruise. Becky was 42 and worked at the Pentagon. We met on a fan site for our favorite TV show, *The L Word.* When Becky found out an episode would be filmed on a ship she called me right away. The cruise would also host a lesbian film festival, a concert by Shawn Colvin, and one by the Indigo Girls. A Halloween party, contest, and presidential election party also topped the itinerary. The ship left from Tampa, Florida and stopped in Key West, and two places in Mexico before heading back to Tampa. I couldn't miss this opportunity.

First, I needed to tell Mom I planned to take a trip with a friend I had only met online. Then, I couldn't tell her the cruise was gay, because I hadn't come out. Growing up with little experience besides dating guys (without having sex), I was still in an exploratory state. The only term I could use was bi-sexual or bi-curious, but I didn't want to tell her that, either. I would tell her I was a fan of the TV show, but the TV show was quite provocative. Luckily my mother hadn't seen it or heard of it.

"It's like *Will and Grace,*" I said, describing the show to her when she stopped over to my place one weekend. I lied since *Will and Grace* was a comedy on regular TV with no gay women, only gay men.

She bought it.

"And it's a ship with only women; I think some are gay because there's a film festival and a few concerts, but it's safer with all women," I said trying to convince her. "My friend works at the Pentagon, Mom. She's safe. I talked to her on the phone many times."

"Well, that sounds fun, but maybe you should meet her first," Mom said.

Was I finally at the point in my life when my mother realized I was an adult and going to make my own decisions? I evolved from needing her permission to wanting her to condone my decisions. And when your mother is on the same side as you the world feels balanced.

A few months later October brought the anticipated cruise. Becky and I met at the airport. She was shorter than I expected and her blonde hair and pretty blue eyes couldn't mask her extra body weight. Yet I couldn't blame her for her appearance. She spent most of her twenties in the hospital. Doctors couldn't figure out what was wrong with her. She had a few surgeries, one removing one of her intestines. After surgery she had terrible pains in her chest and stomach. They took an x-ray but found nothing. Becky suffered a long time until another scan finally caught the sponge they left in her. The lawsuit paid for her Master's Degree.

Becky had spent a decade sick. She was overly ready to enjoy life.

Becky's wits, extensive knowledge, and humor made her a great travel companion and friend. I loved to pick her brain for information. Becky had never been with a woman before, either, but knew she was gay.

She had come out to her mother when she was 40 while parking their car at a mall.

"I don't think you're straight," her mother said.

"I know, Mom. That's what I've been trying to tell you."

"No, I mean I don't think you parked straight."

"Oh," Becky laughed. Her mother had accepted who she was.

We arrived at the hotel in Tampa for a pre-cruise party. Though I expected not to see any men, the atmosphere surprised me. I glanced around, seeing palm trees, torches, and women in many shapes, sizes, races, ages, hairdos, and fashions. We all stood in the Florida heat. A breeze came off the bay and Tampa's bright nightlife flooded the darkness. The only male I saw, the D.J., played music for our group of over 100 women.

I have always felt different from everyone else in a group. I felt I didn't belong with the beautiful girls in school because I focused intently on my imperfections. I felt different from all the comic geeks at the International

Comic Convention because I hid my geekiness better than they did. And now I felt different from everyone in this room because I didn't feel 100% gay.

The gay cruise, called *Olivia,* was my eighth cruise, yet my first gay cruise. I didn't know what to expect; I had never even gone to a gay bar before. The only other time I spent that many days around that many women was at Girl Scout Camp. This wasn't in any way close to that.

The more I looked around, the more overwhelmed I became. There were women everywhere and they stared at me as men would in a bar. Did some of them want me like that? I had never had sex or had that desire. At the time of this trip I had kissed two girls. I had no interest in either, but I was still curious about women.

As I looked around at the women I wished I fit in. I only belonged in the hallway between the "straight room" and the "gay room." I hoped I would feel different on the ship since we were stuck on it for seven days.

The next day Becky and I boarded the ship. It was a normal-sized cruise ship from Holland America. It had many decks and several pools and bars. The hallways had numerous doors like a hotel, but were long and skinny and extended so far it looked like you were in one of those mirror mazes. After dropping off our luggage we went straight to the casting area. In one room producers were casting for extras in *The L Word.* I waited in line and memorized the lines. Becky waited in the hall for me. When I walked in the tiny room the directors stared at me and didn't say anything. I waited for them to say start or cue me.

"Do you know the line?" one asked, annoyed.

"Oh, I didn't know you wanted me to start," I said, now extra nervous.

Another one pushed the script on their table closer to me. I stood in front of a long table with four women on the other side. Now I felt I didn't belong in this room either; I wasn't an actress, especially with this stage fright.

I had memorized the line but it lay in front of me, distracting me. I tried to say the line yet kept looking at the paper as I said it.

I sucked.

They asked me if I'd be a stand-in for one of the actors because I had the same body size and height. I said I would.

The directors ended up choosing another person to stand in because it was an intimate couple scene. The couple they chose, Lizzie and Shelby from

Michigan, were a cute, femme couple Becky and I had met earlier. Lizzie was fit and tan with brown hair while Shelby looked exactly like Uma Thurman: skinny, blonde, and high cheekbones.

The next day they filmed the scene with the lines I tried out for, which they had given to a tall black woman with dreadlocks. Becky and I found our way into the background of the scene, but later I noticed I got cut out of the shot.

The rest of the filming that day was of dancing by the pool. The pool was lighter cerulean blue than the ocean whose view disappeared below the railings when you sat down on one of the white lounge chairs; though with so many people standing, the chairs weren't visible either. Becky was off somewhere talking to a new friend. I danced with Lizzie and Shelby. We were dancing on camera when Shelby leaned down to kiss Lizzie and Lizzie pulled away.

"I don't want anyone from my work to see me on this show," she said, obviously not "out" at work. Shelby cared less what people thought.

I started to feel more comfortable in this group until a woman took off her shirt to reveal a naked chest full of tattoos. I looked away.

The sun sailed in and out of tiny clouds and the breeze by the side of the pool cooled down the crowd of bikinis, sunglasses, drinks, and buzz cuts.

We danced for what seemed like a half hour. Then the director said, "Cut!"

"Everyone has to stop singing 'Girls Just Wanna Have Fun' because we may not get the rights for that song," the director yelled.

The next shot we had to do without music for sound purposes.

"We can't dance to music?" Lizzie said. "Then they are gonna paste a song over this and we are all gonna be off beat and people are gonna see it and think that lesbians can't dance!"

The next day my anxiety lessened. I flirted with a girl who was completely not interested in me, but it still felt good to flirt. One girl whispered in my ear that I was hot and the nervous feeling came back.

That evening Becky and I hung out in a big group. We met twin sisters who were both gay, Sara and Anna. They were both business women in their 40s, short blonde hair and wore barely any make-up. Anna told Becky that Sara was a player and stole her girlfriends in high school because Sara was prettier than her.

I had always been attracted to older women and thought the hottest actresses in Hollywood were over 40. Older women were more stable in their lives; they knew what they wanted. They were wise, experienced, and in their prime.

My initial attraction wasn't that of romance or sex. It didn't have to do with having a good or bad relationship with my mother. I had the desire for something more on a level I hadn't yet explored.

That night Becky and I went to the Halloween party. Becky didn't care much to dress up. I dressed as Halle Berry's version of Catwoman. Black leather belts crisscrossed my back and open waist. I cut jagged holes in my pewter-colored vinyl pants. My shoulder-length hair, which was at that time blonde, I stuffed into a black nylon mask with cat ears. High heels made me over 6 feet tall and my bright red lipstick accented my full lips. My Victoria's Secret bra in leopard print pushed up my tiny breasts. I was now a target for the single ladies *and* the committed ones. Becky and I watched the Halloween costume contest. With all the stares, tongue gestures, and whispers towards me I felt uncomfortable enough to change out of Catwoman. Becky waited for me in the bar.

I spent the next evening in the dance club on the ship. The ship had a few bars and nightclubs, but the one on the top deck was the most popular. It had a view of the ocean, of course, dark, but lit with various colors of lights that ran around the room like a disco. Red, green, and blue dots climbed up the walls and flew across the ceiling. The bar was a half circle, small and intimate. Music played in the background and the lights seemed to move to the beat.

Shelby came up to me and pointed at a feminine-looking, slender-bodied girl who had asked her about me. I confidently walked up to the girl. Her name was Darlene.

"Were you Catwoman last night?" she asked. The rainbow-colored lights of the club flashed around us.

"How did you know?" I asked because I wore a mask.

"The shape of your lips," she said.

She sounded more honest than trying to flirt. Her goofiness was cute and charming. Darlene looked younger than her age, 33, and her long, blonde hair shone with a reddish tone. She was a graphic designer from the East Coast.

Darlene told me her coming out story, which was not so different from the path I was on.

Darlene had never been attracted much to men, yet was nervous meeting women. It took her a while to finally explore her sexual side with a woman.

I didn't know if I was ready for that.

By now I had met many gay people and heard their coming out stories, each so different. Some stories were sad, yet powerful. It's hard not to have sympathy for people struggling just to be themselves. I then understood the meaning of gay pride. It's not that people are just proud to be gay, but they're proud for standing up and being who they truly are, especially when it's so difficult.

Darlene and I kissed and danced and talked. Her sandy blonde strands tickled my cheeks. And every time we kissed her teeth hit mine and she moved her body in a strange circular motion that wasn't sexy. I said good night and went back to my room. Later she called and we made plans to meet up the following afternoon at 4 after our day in Mexico. I enjoyed the attention and experimentation.

The next day we docked at Progresso, Mexico by a cruise ship full of old retired couples. I watched them as they looked out at the ocean, then at our ship. It was amusing to see some of them realize what they were seeing. The old men did double takes when they noticed the couples kissing and holding hands were both women. One old man even took out binoculars.

After climbing and sketching Mayan ruins with Becky, 4 p.m. quickly approached. I arrived a couple of minutes late for the date, but Becky had said anything under ten was on time. I waited for twenty-five minutes. Darlene didn't show. I had been stood up. My rumbling stomach took me to the buffet for food.

The dining area had a large buffet with a variety of cuisines. I sat down by a couple in their 40s. "Gosh, where is everyone?" I asked, looking around at the near empty room.

"Oh we don't know. Seems they are all off doing something. I guess there was a time change when we arrived in Mexico."

"Really? What time is it? Must be an hour early! I didn't get stood up! I can still make my date," I said looking at the time, nearly 5, or what should be 4.

They laughed as I set my drink down and ran upstairs. 5 came, then 5:15. Now she's late, I thought. Or had I gotten stood up twice for the same date?

Ten minutes later she showed up and apologized. She, too, had been confused about the time. I smiled, glad I hadn't been stood up. My knee-length black skirt blew up in the wind. A fake pink flower barrette held my hair behind one ear. Darlene's tight purple tank top revealed her small waist. She wore khaki shorts and sandals. Her lilac eye shadow said 80s nostalgia.

Darlene and I hung out and ended up in the club on the top deck. We sat at the bar and Darlene went to the bathroom. I realized going to the bathroom is not a possible intermission during a date with the same sex, as we share a bathroom and women usually go there together.

Darlene seemed to be gone for a long time. A woman approached me.

"I see you have a bump on your nose, like me," she said. I wasn't flattered since I hated the bump on my nose. It somewhat resembled the Native American profile in Southwestern paintings; though I probably couldn't attribute it to my 3% Native American heritage.

"I'm Geena," she said, extending her hand politely.

"Hi, I think I recognize you from one of the movies I saw playing on the ship," I said. Geena had a Greek, rebellious Jackie Kennedy look to her with a fit body, and an alike bump in her nasal profile.

Finally Darlene came back from the bathroom. "This is Geena, from one of the films," I said, introducing her. Darlene wasn't impressed; in fact, she looked pissed. Geena asked if I wanted to dance, and I did, so I tried to pull Darlene out on the dance floor. Darlene resisted. I gestured to get her to come but she became more upset. I didn't know what to do, so I kept dancing with Geena.

Geena's sporty tank top was a mix of blue and purple and sat just above her black mini skirt. She seemed to be the type who preferred jeans.

"Who's your favorite actress besides yourself?" I asked her.

"I'm actually a comedian; that was my first film. I like Susan Sarandon," she yelled into my ear because of the loud music.

"Me, too!"

We moved to the beat of the techno dance music without touching.

"Ah, maybe I'll see ya later," I said and went back to Darlene.

Darlene wouldn't talk to me or look at me. Finally she turned around and said, "You wouldn't do that if you were on a date with a guy."

What was she talking about? What did I do? I had tried to get her to dance and she wouldn't. I thought we were just hanging out so we could both dance with Geena. Was this a real date? Was Geena trying to be with me? This confused me. I rubbed Darlene's back but she never turned around, mumbled something about me being a player and obsessed with celebrities. With no more response from her I left. I saw Anna on my way out sitting at the bar. I needed advice.

I poured out my problems to Anna. She explained that when you're on a date, you don't leave your partner and go dance with another woman. But it also felt like Darlene was a jealous person and had overreacted. This gay world wasn't going to be easy. I wasn't even used to guys asking me out in bars or anything of the sort. I wanted a real girlfriend; that was my goal.

The next morning Becky and I hung out in the lounge. A glass chandelier hung from the two-story ceiling and the walls held large overpriced artwork for sale. I sketched while we chatted. Darlene and her friends were visible from a distance and they all glared at me except Darlene. I didn't care. If she was going to be that jealous I didn't want her. And she was a bad kisser, anyway.

The 2004 presidential election occurred while we cruised at sea. At the party I saw Jane Lynch (She's mostly known now for acting in the TV show *Glee*). At the time I didn't know she was gay, but knew she had played a lesbian in the movie *Best in Show*. Jane's shirt said, "Wax Bush". I guess the other lesbians didn't follow her as we found out most voted for Bush. Why? Then I figured it out. Most of the women were business women in their 40s. They wanted their money from the Republicans more than they wanted their gay rights from the Democrats.

The last night Becky teased me about Geena and I teased her about her crush on the marketing director for Showtime she had met on the ship. Becky and I went to the top deck club and tried to hook someone up with shy Anna. No luck. Geena came over and danced with me for a bit. I wanted to know more about her, talk to her, have a conversation; yet I said goodnight because we had to pack and get up early.

"I'll be here all night," she said.

I went with Becky back to our tiny room to pack. We lay in our beds, the space between barely big enough to walk to our bathroom, which was right by the door. How larger people maneuver in these microscopic bathrooms I didn't know.

28

Becky's snores became louder as I lay in bed. Each one broke my concentration on my struggle between sleep and Geena. I had to go back up there. Geena was waiting and curiosity killed me.

I got up and snuck out during snores as to not wake Becky, though I don't think much could have awoken her at that point.

I wore my black tank top and black pants. I saw Geena in her shorts and white tank top. She stood right in the place I left her, now with Jane Lynch and Jane's girlfriend.

"This is Jane," Geena said, introducing me to her.

"Hi, I'm Jane," Jane said, as she shook my hand.

"I know," was all I could say, because I did know who she was. Does Angelina Jolie go around and say, "Hi, I'm Angelina." Duh, who doesn't know you?

It was the first time I had been formally introduced to a celebrity.

Geena wanted to dance so we did. Then she whispered, "You wanna get out of here?" I nodded.

We ran around the ship hand in hand, her, a 43-year-old, experienced, semi-famous lesbian, and me, a 23-year-old virgin. We talked a bit out on the windy deck. I asked her what her second career choice would be. She told me weather patterns interested her and I told her I found astronomy fascinating. You could barely see the ocean in the darkness. The wind blew hard. I felt excited and free. Who was this amazing woman who was interested in me?

We left the deck and attended the late night lecture going on about the first major lesbian film, *Desert Hearts*, by the director herself. We listened for a while, then I kissed Geena on our way out and she kissed me back. We ran down the hallway, obviously going toward her room.

"Are you okay with this?" she said. Was there something I might not be okay with? Now I was nervous, but nothing stopped me from following her to her room. Her room, much larger than Becky's and my room, encased a giant bed in the center. We talked about the death of Geena's mom and my dad. I remembered Becky saying how comedy comes out of grief. Perhaps that's why Geena became a comedian.

Geena went to the bathroom and stayed longer than I expected. I had time to figure out what I should do. Should I lie on the bed? Take my clothes off? Sit on the chair?

When she finally came out I decided to act out a scene from *Desert Hearts* right before the younger woman seduces the older woman. She caught on and finished the scene with the innocent, almost old-fashioned, words that passed in 70s cinema for foreplay.

We started kissing. She kissed like a professional, maybe because she had the most experience of anyone I had kissed. And, in contrast to the last girl, almost anyone would have been better. Her nipples were as soft as baby skin and I took advantage of kissing them.

"Do you wanna take off your pants?" she asked.

I shook my head, scared. She rubbed her naked body on my pants. Then I thought, screw it, and took my pants off, still leaving my black underwear on. I didn't know what she wanted me to do, but my finger found the right place. I loved a woman's body artistically and comfortingly, and now, I loved it sexually, too.

Everything made sense. I was born this way and I felt comfortable with who I was; however, I still couldn't say it out loud. It wasn't until I was on an airplane with Momtom on our yearly ski trip to Salt Lake City that the words just spilled out.

<u>Winter 2004</u>

"It's a bad sign when the safety video doesn't work," I remembered a guy saying on a previous flight. Luckily the safety video on this flight was working.

I watched the video though I could probably have recited it by now having seen it over 100 times. As the plane took off my mother held my hand tight, as was our tradition whenever we flew. We let go when the plane was up and steady. Mom took out her travel rosary and began to pray, her daily routine.

We were headed to Salt Lake City to ski.

One time when we were flying home from Salt Lake with family, there was a loud noise and the plane started to get smoky. A flight attendant ran up the aisle and asked us to feel the floor for heat. When other passengers looked around with panic, my mother sat calmly. She made me feel at ease in a potentially deadly situation. Mom told me she knew it wasn't her time to go.

"The family that flies together, dies together," my uncle said on the flight.

"You can't wait till we're on the ground to make a joke like that!" His wife said, yelling at him and trying to tell the 12-year-old girl next to her flying alone to stop screaming and shut up. One man started having a panic attack.

On this flight to Salt Lake, Mom sat as calmly like she had on the horrific flight, in the middle seat with her head back, eyes closed, lips moving forming the words of the rosary. She held the tiny ring of ten beads and one cross between the thumb and fingers of her right hand.

"We have reached an altitude where you may use electronic devices with the exception of cellular phones, TVs, and radios," the flight attendant said in a monotone yet pretty voice.

I reached for my headphones and CDs.

When Mom finished silently reciting her daily prayers she pulled out her stash of various candies: Peppermint patty balls, M&Ms, and mint Lifesavers. They appeared during road trips, plane trips, and movies in theaters. I shared her treats and gave her some of mine: chocolate covered pretzels, pistachios, and Smarties.

Tom closed his eyes, yet refrained from his usual snoring.

My mother's short hair, dyed red, stuck to the side of her head where she rested on the plane seat. It had grown out since chemo treatments ended and she had dyed it red for Tom.

I could never lie to my mother, not for very long. I knew it was going to come out soon enough, but I hadn't planned for it at this moment and had no back-up plan.

It slipped out like an unexpected burp.

"Mom, ah, I'm gay…and so is Becky." I held my breath.

My mom looked at the seat in front of Tom, who now awoke.

Scared to look at her face, I distracted myself with the exit instructions. Plus the seats faced forward, so turning my head and looking at her would've been awkwardly too close.

I pictured the plane filling with smoke.

People sat behind us chatting softly, whispering. About me? I looked around. Did the people in front of me just hear that? Did the people beside me? The people behind me? Of course they did. The inside of the plane looked smaller and smaller. I wanted to leave but realized the only place to escape was the bathroom and you couldn't stay there for long. I noticed the barf bag in the seat pocket. I hoped my mother couldn't see my face turning red.

"Ok," my mom said slowly, as if she was still processing what I said.

Silence. More whispering, then silence. Was everyone waiting for me to speak?

"You know that cruise Becky and I went on last month? Well, I was intimate with someone on the ship." I held my breath again. My throat dried up. Why did I always feel the need to tell all the details like I did when I was a child? Where was the flight attendant with water? Why didn't I think before I spoke? I could tell my mother relatively anything, but I felt like I was being recorded or telling my secrets to a jury because of all the people around us.

"Oh," she said softly, still listening, and perhaps aware everyone around us was listening. "Are you dating someone now?"

My mother sat stoically, almost creepily, like a mannequin in a chair. She closed her eyes and leaned her head back. I looked at Tom from the corner of my eye. He pretended not to listen, though I knew he always did.

I started to whisper more now, yet I felt as if everyone's ears were strained, listening.

"Yes," I said.

The long pauses between responses sneered at me.

"What does she do?" Mom asked.

"She's going to college in Minnesota to be an English Professor," I said, proud.

"She's pretty," my mom said looking at the dark-haired Mexican girl from Texas I had met online. I was comfortable dating a woman, but not yet comfortable to tell the world beyond my friends and family. I put the photograph away and Mom closed her eyes.

What was she thinking? Maybe she was picturing the plane filling with smoke too.

I had started dating my first girlfriend, Ellie. She was 34, tall, fit, and her geeky smartness made her more attractive. She had a passion for obnoxious looking shoes that took people's attention away from her shyness. Bright purple heels with lacy yellow sides topped her favorites. Like me, she had one cat and a passion for writing.

32

I kept waiting for some kind of approval from my mother, but she only sat there quietly. I tried to think of something I could say to get a reaction.

"So, did I surprise you?" I asked.

"Oh, I don't know," she said. "Well, you don't have to make any decisions about anything now."

Maybe she thought I was confused, thought it was a phase. This was going to be a process. I couldn't sit still, wondering what my mother thought. What was in her head that she wasn't saying? I knew Mom still loved me, but would she treat me differently? I wanted her to condone me. I wanted her to be on the same side of my tilted world.

When our horrific, smoke-filled flight had landed safely back in Salt Lake to change planes, we found out the problem was a faulty air conditioning system that created smoke. When we landed we were given a free food voucher which most people used for a beer.

I was too young back then to drink, but I could've really used a beer now, as it was a long, silent plane ride to Utah.

My mother had asked me my first year of college if I was gay. Surprised, I asked her why. She answered, "You have pictures of actresses on your walls, you talk about your friends that are gay, and you always say you'll never find the perfect guy."

I told her no. I had thought the pictures of actresses meant I wanted to be pretty like them. Gay friends were common when you attended an art college. And the perfect guy really doesn't exist. I thought I would wait till marriage to have sex. I didn't know why I never felt comfortable dating a guy. I didn't know sex with a man was something I would never want.

In time my body told me what sexual feelings were normal for me. It wasn't until then that my adolescence made more sense; my closeness to women and my aversion to dating men.

Later that evening in Salt Lake City I sat down in the office to work on the book I was illustrating for a client, "99 Ways to Use a Wedding Gown (After the Honeymoon-or the Marriage-is Over)." Mom was in there organizing papers at her desk. She had just vacuumed the house, even though it sat vacant for a year without use and was still clean.

"Tom says he thinks you're dating women because you want to have sex and it's wrong to have sex before marriage with a guy," Mom said, unexpectedly. I saw Tom walk by. His small but noticeable beer belly reminded me he wasn't as skinny as he looked from behind.

"Okay, ah, well that's not it," I said, embarrassed Tom had an opinion on my sex life. Tom went to church with my mother so I shouldn't have been shocked at his Catholic way of thinking. I decided to go downstairs to my bedroom to work.

My mother's talent at interior decorating was exhibited throughout the rambler with a Southwestern theme. Kokopellis danced on the walls. Silhouettes of wolves howled at the moon next to pictures of cacti and clay pots. The quilts on the beds matched the wall décor and anything that could have a fabric-sewn cover that matched, my mother made for it. Every room in the house that had a window had a view of mountains. I would love to live here if my entire family and friends didn't live back in Minnesota.

Later during our vacation in Utah we went out for dinner. Mom was in a giggly mood and Tom left to go to the bathroom.

Out of nowhere my mother said, "So are you the guy or the girl?"

"What?" I said confused for a moment. Then I chuckled. "Mom, we are both women."

She laughed and then said seriously, "I know what you mean. Even with your dad we were equal on things. He had quite a few feminine qualities and we shared a lot of responsibilities."

Tom came back to the table. I was so happy my mom had started to accept and understand, until Ellie and I visited at Easter.

Easter 2005

My mother wanted to set up her youngest brother, Pete. Pete was nearing 45 and had never been married. He was a handsome and honest guy, but his lack of finances and habit of drinking kept him from being an eligible bachelor. Easter Sunday Mom invited Tom's youngest sister, who was single, and I brought Ellie and my best friend from college, Yolanda. Since Uncle Pete had a history of dating skinny women, I knew Yolanda wouldn't be his type.

At Easter, Ellie met my mom for the first time. My mother was so distracted by her guests that there wasn't much interaction besides a polite hello. I hadn't told anyone else in the family Ellie was my girlfriend, so I couldn't complain that Mom treated Ellie no differently from Yolanda. Ellie didn't like showing affection in front of anyone so we only looked like friends.

Yolanda's loveable, obnoxious laugh and round figure contrasted with Ellie's demure smile and tiny ankles. Ellie wore a copper cross necklace and a black dress that matched her medium length hair. Instead of her black frame glasses, she opted for contacts.

We played some card games with my aunts and uncles, ate, and left.

After, Mom asked Uncle Pete if there were any girls he was interested in. He said maybe.

Later that week Pete called, asking me for Ellie's number. I told him she was with someone. He even asked about her again a few months later, not knowing we had broken up. I was so mad my mother had to make a big deal out of the "single girls" and my uncle had to pick my girlfriend!

I called Mom.

"Mom, why did you have to keep asking Pete about the girls when you knew Ellie was my girlfriend? You were pushing him and you knew he was going to pick her!"

"I didn't know he was going to pick her," she laughed and giggled like it was all a joke to her.

She wouldn't understand, so I stopped trying. I focused less on my mother's actions and more on my relationship with Ellie.

A month later I broke up with Ellie. Even though she was beautiful, smart, and good to me, I wasn't ready for the serious relationship it seemed she wanted. I hoped she'd stick around, but she was heartbroken and disappeared from my life. I didn't like hurting her, but I didn't know what I wanted with my life and my career and wanted to be free.

When I told Mom, she said, "So because it didn't work out that lifestyle's probably not for you." I didn't respond to that. It seemed like she wanted my gay days to be over, which disappointed me; because my gay days had just begun.

Over the next five years I transitioned from dating guys and girls to solely girls. My relationship with my mother was distant during those times as we were both focused on our own lives. Mom married Tom, traveled a lot, and was more involved in church and her retired lifestyle.

My lifestyle contained dozens of freelance and part-time jobs, outings with friends, traveling, art projects, moving, and long-distant commuting for relationships. Even though I wanted to date women I wasn't sure I was completely ready to give up opportunities with men. So, I dated a few guys before I realized I wasn't bisexual. As I was usually in between jobs, houses, religions, and sexualities, I understood my mother's distance from me. "I think that's why I don't like people in their 20s much. They are so unsettled," she had said to me once.

It took me until I dated a guy and a girl at the same time before I realized I was truly gay and no man could change me. It explains a lot when the guy I'm dating doesn't even get a kiss and the girl I'm dating gets 2nd base and a sleepover. I realized I had always been gay I just didn't know what those feelings meant when I was growing up.

By age 29 I was finally ready to settle down, and ready to tell my mother this gay life was permanent. Anything wonderful in my life, Mom was the first to know. And now that I had found my life partner, Donna, I had to tell my mother. I wanted for Mom to meet Donna and be more a part of my life. But because this would confirm to her that I was truly gay and not going to change, it was as if I had to come out to her again. Maybe it was her more extreme dedication to Catholicism and our lack of closeness, but I felt more nervous than before.

Summer 2010

I drove to my mother's house and sat in her sewing room, waiting for her to finish her project. The room contained many sewing supplies and leftover projects, but it was far from messy as my mother was the most organized person I knew. Brightly colored pincushions hid in slightly open drawers. Numerous rolls of thread filled up a shelf, each sitting upright and organized by color. Plastic containers with labels sat stacked in the wall-sized cabinet. Dust from thread and lint piled nicely in the white ceramic trashcan like it had collected itself magically by the snap of a finger.

The TV uttered a show she had taped. It didn't matter that it was 2010, or that I had bought her a TiVo, Mom still insisted on recording TV shows on VHS tapes.

I made some small talk, so she turned off the show. Sewing was so natural for her yet she looked focused as she used the Serger to finish off the end of the fabric. We had to talk in between times she used the Serger as it sounded like a machine chopping up vegetables on high speed.

"Ah, I met someone online," I said.

She kept working on her project.

"It's a woman. Her name is Donna. I'm really serious about her."

She cut the thread with a scissor.

"I'm very sure of myself, Mom. I know I'm gay."

The sound of the Serger grew loud and fast.

I swallowed twice.

Silence.

"Ok, what do you want me to say?" she asked.

"I just wanted to tell you."

"She's pretty. What does she do?" Mom asked as she glanced at the photo on my phone I help up of a beautiful Vietnamese woman in a pink shirt with a white coat.

"She works for Homeland Security and has an eight-year-old son," I said.

I kept the fact that she had a motorcycle to myself for the time being. I knew Mom thought motorcycles were dangerous. Mom's salmon colored t-shirt hid the few pounds she had been trying to lose for a year now.

The pedal of the Serger squeaked as it activated the annoying chopping sound.

"Were you and Becky together?" Mom asked.

I was surprised she remembered Becky and thought that.

"No," I said, "We were just friends."

"How do you feel about your faith in the church?" She finally asked what I knew was on her mind.

Though my mother was very Catholic, she was also very open. She didn't believe everything the church said. I was proud of her for using her own mind and experiences when it came to beliefs. She grew up with a gay uncle, my great uncle, Leon. He was such a loveable man that his family was able to embrace him instead of shun him. I'm grateful to him for being out and making it easier for me. I wished AIDS hadn't killed him when I was 10.

"I have a relationship with God and I know that these feelings of love I have are not wrong. God isn't showing me they are wrong. I don't think I will go to hell for loving someone."

"Ok, if that's how you feel. I just want you to have a relationship with God, honey," she said.

"I do."

We walked into the kitchen and she called for Tom to help her with dinner.

"She has a son, though. You won't be able to travel much," my mother said.

"I don't care, I love her," I said. "Dad had kids, too and you said you knew right away he was the one."

"Yes, I did."

I reached for the plates from the cabinet and set them down on the deep blue marble countertop.

"I would like to meet Donna someday," she said, finally telling me what I wanted to hear.

I smiled to myself and glanced at the frozen broccoli and corn Mom pulled out of the freezer. I was now used to the freshly grown vegetables, fried pork, and jasmine rice that Donna's family cooked.

"Set the table," she said.

Food

Deciding on food for the wedding was a bit difficult. Donna preferred Asian food, but most of the guests would be American. We compromised on a mix. At the ceremony we would have Asian-style cake, pork dumplings, spring rolls, egg rolls, stir fry noodles with vegetables, four cheese spreads with crackers, vegetable pastry cake, crab dip, and bread with hummus. For the entrée choices at the reception we picked lemongrass chicken with rice and salmon with wasabi mashed potatoes.

I believed in true love at first sight when I met Donna. That's why I proposed only a week after we met. She was my ideal type; a foreign woman, feminine, with an athletic body, a mother with a protective nature and job. I liked women with kids because they weren't as selfish, having someone on this planet to live for besides themselves.

Donna was the one I had been searching for, but thought I would never find.

I didn't remember until many months into our relationship that I had had a vision of Donna. When I studied poetry in Italy I visited Verona, Shakespeare's *Romeo and Juliet* city of love. The opera that night was "Madame Butterfly," the operatic version of "Miss Saigon." The story of "Miss Saigon" follows a Vietnamese woman who falls in love with an American and has a son and wants to come to America with the one she loves. It was that night in an open-air opera arena under the stars in the city of lovers I wished for true love to find me. Miss Saigon had found me just two months later. She understood my humor. Her beauty overwhelmed me. Donna was the one.

Photos of Donna's motorcycle and her in a security uniform with her gun thrilled me. Who doesn't like a woman in uniform? She strongly valued family and shared my dreams of traveling and having another child. I enjoyed the diversity of culture and language and learning first-hand about another place on this earth.

Donna and I danced together, worked out together, and played cards together. She taught me Vietnamese, how to cook Asian food, and various other intricacies about her culture.

Having a knack and passion for languages, I was motivated to learn Vietnamese as quickly as possible. Within just a few days of knowing each other, one evening Donna said to me, "Yêu em." Without knowing much, I knew what she said; I felt it too. She told me she loved me.

Donna had been with a few women before, after her ten-year marriage to a man, but no one serious. When I first met Donna, she had been looking for a house for herself and her eight-year-old son Todd, who would live with her half the week and the other half with his dad. It only seemed rational for Donna and I to look for a big enough place that would fit my stuff too, cats and all.

Two months into our relationship Donna and I went house hunting. We hadn't been together that long, yet we were ready for commitment. A house together would also solve the issue of driving a half hour when her family needed her; or me going to her place which was already crowded with her son, ex-husband, parents, her sister's family from Vietnam who had three children, and sometimes her brothers. We wanted to be alone and be a family. Some of our friends called us crazy, but we knew what we wanted.

Fall 2010

Donna and I sat in the back of the realtor's car. The once-clean tan interior showed off its Coke or Pepsi stains. I tried to ignore them as the realtor's leftover tuna sandwich smell drifted into the back. Donna put the window down for air, but then put it up when she heard my phone ring.

The realtor, Shirley, slammed on the breaks and Donna and I lunged forward.

"Oops, stop sign," Shirley said with an apologetic giggle.

Donna caught my eye, as this was the fourth time that day Shirley had almost broken driving laws.

My phone waited for an answer.

"Wow, look at that house," Donna said, pointing.

I pushed the green button. The car continued to drive past green lawns, fences, mailboxes; eventually all became a blur.

"Hi!" I answered, excited to hear her voice.

The car drove on, passing parks and walking paths.

"What?" I asked the phone, not believing. "Is it cancer?"

Donna and Shirley's side conversation about backyards stopped abruptly.

Donna's long black hair lay in a ponytail on her back beneath her blue baseball cap. When Donna ran out of things to say, Shirley filled up the silence like she always did with chatter. When Shirley looked at me in the rear view mirror she knew it was more serious.

"We can head back to the office," she said.

"My mom has a tumor in her skull," I said, when I was able to talk.

Donna's eyes widened but she tried to hide it as she put one hand on my knee and one on my back. I used the sleeve of my sweatshirt as Kleenex.

"No, let's go see the last house. I need to keep my mind off things," I said.

"Are you sure?" Donna asked worried, rubbing my leg. Her short jean shorts revealed much of her tan, muscular thighs.

"Yes, I'm sure. Can we please go see it, Shirley?"

"Of course," Shirley said, her voice back to cheery.

Shirley was a very overweight woman, short and round. Her cheeks were big and poofy and inviting. She laughed a lot, especially with Donna and me. I liked her, but she talked too long and too much about realty business issues we didn't care to know. I liked the fact, though, that her husband was from the former Yugoslavia and that she, like I would someday, had a mother-in-law who didn't speak English. Donna's Vietnamese parents had lived in Minnesota since they came with Donna in 1994, but didn't speak any English.

I calmed enough to explain my personal life in front of Shirley.

"My mom has been having headaches for a while, and some double vision. We were supposed to meet up with my stepdad's daughters for his 50th birthday in Oregon next weekend," I said, smelling the exhaust out the window that Donna had put down to get some air in the back.

The sunlight coming in the car faded away. The cancer storm was back.

"They were in Utah. Mom went to the hospital for scans. There's some mass in her skull. They are driving back home now for her to see her usual doctors and have more tests," I said, as if speaking about painful topics was a motor function.

It was Utah again. It had been in Utah that my dad had been told he had three to five months to live because of pancreatic cancer. Now my 59-year-old mother relived the bad news in the same hospital. And the bad news would ride along on the 22-hour drive home. Death with a bow wrapped around it, a black bow of thorns. How much was she remembering of my father? Now she was the one sick and unknowing, unsure of what her prognosis would be. The sentence of death just wouldn't leave this family alone; not for a year, not for five years.

A particular song by Dido helped me through many of the formidable days when my father was dying. The lyrics are: *You're asking me why pain's the only way to happiness. But I promise you you'll see the sun again.* I made a promise to myself that I would see happy days again. I would wait for the sun. And that's what got me through.

"It will be okay, honey, it could be nothing," Donna said.

Her comfort didn't work. I knew cancer too well. My mom's friend had died of a brain tumor a few years ago. They had given her steroids till her face ballooned up. Then she died anyway. And our accountant had died last year. She was 52 and her breast cancer had spread to her brain. She had left her two teenage daughters behind. I wasn't ready to be an orphan at 29. Couldn't I at least get to 35 without losing the only immediate family I had?

I walked into the house Shirley showed us, not caring and not seeing. My mother's health consumed my mind.

On the way back to the office, Shirley made a wrong turn.

"Oopsies," she said giggling, but less this time.

I wanted out of this car, out of this place where bad news littered the air. All I could do was wait. Waiting for tests, waiting for answers, waiting for stoplights, waiting for my next breath…waiting for the sun.

After my mom returned home and had more tests, I drove the hour to her house for dinner. Mom never told me information right when I walked in the door. There had to be an informal greeting, and some iced tea that was watered down to barely a taste, the way we both liked it. There had to be some quiet time when the phone wasn't ringing or the news wasn't on, sometime between dinner and feeding the cat; time for a burden of news, the receiving of the gift with the black thorn bow.

My stomach tightened beneath the muscles I forced myself to use to breathe. I wasn't hungry. I hadn't been hungry the night they told me Dad was sick. It's that moment that cuts the red ribbon of happiness you had throughout childhood if you were lucky.

Mom said we would go out for dinner. She didn't feel like cooking, either. Go out to celebrate the bad news? I guess it was easier to hide emotion in public.

42

Mom sat in her forest green soft chair in the living room. I sat on the edge of the pastel pink chaise lounge. Both were taken so well care of for years that they looked brand new. I tried to sit in the chair in a relaxed position, but it was impossible. This was worse than the first time. I was seven years older yet somehow it was worse. Before, it had been breast cancer. Something that could be removed. And they removed it. However, they couldn't remove my mother's skull. Was it cancer? Please no.

"Ok, just tell me," I said, waiting for the bullet I had tried to accept.

"I have a small mass in my skull in the bone. They also saw a spot on my hip. It's really tiny but they still want to do radiation. The oncologist said it's the breast cancer coming back as bone cancer."

I took a short, quick breath. The room screamed the word *cancer* at me till my ears rang. Cancer of the bones was bad. My great uncle had died of it. I remember people saying how excruciating it was. I couldn't imagine my mother in that much pain. I watched her part her lips to speak, my mind fighting not to shut down.

"The oncologist is really optimistic. The radiation treatment is very effective. They will keep testing me and giving me medication, and if something new pops up they will treat it. But I may never be cured. It will be up and down like a roller coaster for a long time."

I couldn't take this constant up and down, not knowing when you're going to be sick to the point of dying or sick to the point of living. Trying not to cry, and unsure if I wanted to hold her or I wanted her to hold me, my body moved to her chair as I reached for her hand.

"I'm not ready to lose you yet," I said.

All the sorrow I had avoided during my dad's death, all the sorrow I had bypassed when my mother first got cancer piled up on top of me now. I was alone again; not safe from the clouds overhead. Where was the rainbow after the storm, the one that was made of colored ribbons, but never actually made a bow; that promised you the storm was over?

It rained harder and harder and it didn't stop.

There actually was a flash flood warning that night. Donna drove the hour up through the rain to be with me at Mom's, leaving Todd with his father. She didn't want me to be alone that night in my mother's basement, the word *cancer* floating above, devising how it could attack me like an enraged bird. Did my mother feel like it was a bird attacking her? Was it a tiger sitting on her bed, waiting for her to move?

Donna worked security and had to get up at 4 a.m. just to be on time the next day, yet she still came.

I worried about the radiation. What if the radiation was a tiny bit off? What if the wrong part of my mother's skull was irradiated? The tumor was close to her brain; what if the doctors screwed up? I couldn't help but think about those questions.

"What's on your mind?" Donna asked me in Vietnamese one night.

I answered her in English since my Vietnamese was so limited.

"Honey, try not to think about these things. She will be okay. It could be worse," Donna said, kissing my hand in bed.

I guess it could be worse. Everything could be worse. Yet in my mind there was nothing worse than this. However, I understood Donna's mentality.

"Go hug him, that's your father," Donna's mother had told her when she was five. Scared of the dirty, tortured stranger in front of her, Donna still obeyed her mother. Donna didn't see her father again until he was released from prison when she was seven.

Donna's dad had been a Special Agent for the U.S. Government in Vietnam in the 1970s. When Donna was still in her mother's womb, her dad was captured by the Communists and tortured in prison for seven years. Since her father was in prison, her mother worked to support the family. While Donna's mother was gone working to support fourteen family members, Donna's sister took her around to neighbors who could breastfeed Donna.

Their family worked on the farms, sometimes more than 13 hours a day. Donna didn't come to America with her parents until she was 18 years old. Forced to learn English and go to American high school, she went through depression from being away from her culture, country, and sister. Donna had been through hardships I could never imagine. But she hadn't experienced her parents dying at a younger age. She was 35 years old. I would be lucky to still have a mother at 35.

The next week Donna and I left on another house-hunting session with Shirley. Donna and I wanted nothing more than to live together. After all, life seemed shorter every day.

"How's your mom?" Shirley asked politely.

Why did it seem like realtors weaved into the most strenuous times in my family's life?

When my mom's depression was so bad that she didn't talk, there had been a realtor there, too. At 18 years old, I had hated that realtor and the "point of interest" yellow post-its she stuck around the house and on my closet door. My mom had hated her the most, but only because the realtor was the image behind all the changes in life that my mother found too hard to embrace all at once: dad retiring, me graduating, and us moving.

The first encounter I ever had with realtors was when I was five. We were selling our house and a couple came to look at it. I didn't know what was going on, but I knew it was something bad. I played in the backyard while the realtor showed the couple the house. When they came to look in the backyard I sprayed them with the garden hose. My mother yelled at me.

My parents bought a second home in Utah through a realtor. My parents were in Utah when my dad got sick, two years after he retired. Mom was out shopping and didn't have a cell phone. Dad needed someone to take him to the hospital. The only person he knew was the realtor, so Dad called him. Cancer and a realtor: my first major experience of personal heartbreak and misfortune.

Shirley's GPS led us to the wrong house.

"Well that's funny, I thought I typed in the address right," Shirley said, fumbling with papers.

The familiar back seat of bad news smelled of fresh cut grass from the open window. The contrasting smell of my Dr. Pepper calmed me. I rarely drank pop, but I needed something to distract my senses and I hoped it would distract my mind.

"Oh sorry, hold on, my daughter's calling me," Shirley said while starting to drive again.

The drink holders in between the seats put a distance between me and Donna.

"Red light!" Donna said as politely as she could in her Asian accent from the back seat to Shirley's blue-tooth covered ear.

We lunged forward again.

"Oops, sorry guys," Shirley said with the familiar giggle.

Donna and I both took a deep breath. Then we saw it: the beautiful white house on the corner with the big tree.

We escaped the smelly car and waited by the door for Shirley and her key. Donna and I smiled at each other and gleamed. We loved the fenced-in backyard with a playground for Todd and the daughter we both wanted. The kitchen sold us. Its tall triangle window let the sunlight in to make the kitchen sparkle.

There wasn't an island but there was counter space all around. Brand new stainless steel appliances and a dining room that led out to a nice deck. It immediately felt like home to both of us. Shirley gabbed about something in the other room. Donna and I ignored her, stealing kisses, talking dirty in the kitchen.

We would make this place our home, whatever it took. Life would go on.

As we signed the purchase agreement later, I glanced down at the table in front of us. *We didn't agree to purchase this life of ours. Would I have chosen to buy this life for myself if I knew all the hardships and sadness I would have to face?*

I looked up at Donna's face and I knew the answer: she made my life worth living.

Donna's older sister and her family had come from Vietnam only a year before I met them. They didn't speak English, but the children picked it up fast in school. Her sister, Kay, wasn't comfortable with Donna being gay. Kay stared at me like an eagle, intimidating me when I came to her place to visit.

Once Kay got to know me she started to like me a lot, yet wouldn't admit it. One day I sat with Kay in the hospital waiting room. Donna and Kay's elderly parents had been hospitalized after their yearly trip to Vietnam. They just happened to have a layover on their way back in Tokyo at the moment the 2011 earthquake hit Japan. Twenty minutes after landing they felt the impact of the quake. Stuck there for four days, they became sick from exhaustion and malnutrition.

Kay and I sat waiting for Donna to come back with news after talking to the doctor. The awkwardness of silence from not speaking the same language was ubiquitous. My Vietnamese was limited to conversations about food, sleep, kids, and some naughty phrases Donna taught me. So Kay and I sat silently waiting.

Then I asked Kay if she was tired. She said yes.

She asked me if I thought a girl walking by was pretty. I said yes.

We sat for a while watching the people in the ER come and go.

I asked Kay if she thought another girl was pretty. She said yes.

She asked if I was hungry. I said no.

I asked if she was hungry. She said no.

And so we sat, staring at the floor.

Finally I had an idea. I reached into my purse and pulled out my tiny sketchbook. I started drawing pictures of a house, a car, a shirt, a toilet. I gestured to her to write the word in Vietnamese by the picture. Kay had the same beauty as Donna only most of it was hidden behind lines and years of worry. Her long hair was pulled back and frayed in the ponytail. Her skinny body wore clothes that were rarely new.

Kay wrote down the word and said it so I could pronounce the word and practice. Then Donna came back from her mother's hospital room to find us. I showed Donna what we were doing. She told Kay to draw something. I handed the sketchbook to Kay. Kay said something in Vietnamese and laughed. Kay's immense smile brought life to her face. I looked at the sketchbook. Kay had drawn a penis.

We all laughed. There was no culture or language barrier when it came to drawing penises.

One of the very first drawings I ever did got my parents in trouble.

"I'm concerned about Kelly's drawing," the preschool teacher told my parents when they picked me up.

Both of my parents chuckled when they saw it.

"Sorry," my mother said. "I had just read and shown her a baby birth book."

Even though it was just a circle with a line, it wasn't acceptable in preschool.

"It's a sperm!" I had said, excited, when the teacher had asked me what I had drawn.

This precious, essential circle with a line would be the one thing Donna and I would need to begin our dream of a little family.

A few months after we bought our house, Donna's youngest brother, Vinny, planned to get married. Donna had three brothers who lived here in Minnesota and one was still in Vietnam.

A wedding ceremony in Vietnam is different from an American one. There's a ritual at the boy's house and then they go to the girl's house and have a ceremony there. But Vinny already lived with his fiancée, Connie, and her parents. He was in need of a boy's house if he wanted to do it the Vietnamese traditional way. Since Donna and I had recently moved into a new house that was larger than his other siblings' apartments, he asked if we could do the boy's ceremony at our place. We agreed.

"Make sure your parents come to the wedding," her father told me one night at dinner, translated by Donna.

"Okay," I said. At least "Okay" was universal.

Donna's father didn't approve of her being gay, but he accepted me enough to invite my parents. I felt fortunate until her father's and Vinny's request the day of the wedding.

Summer 2011

"Connie said she ran into some of my friends from high school and invited them to the wedding," Donna told me in the bathroom while we were getting ready for the wedding. "Connie said they asked if I was married and she told them I was. I don't like that she lied like that."

I sat on the side of the tub and listened to her.

"My dad and Vinny want to introduce me as married to my ex. I told them I wouldn't do it."

"What? What do you mean?" I asked.

"The ceremony is videotaped and they send it back to Vietnam and I guess my dad still wants me to be married to Ted."

Donna told me there wasn't really a word in Vietnamese for significant other, partner, girlfriend, or lesbian that translated well for the older generation. People in Vietnam, primarily when her parents lived there, never acknowledged that topic as it was more or less unheard of, especially in the country. I didn't

48

expect her traditional Vietnamese father who was nearly 80 years old to try to find the words for it, but it wasn't right to still pretend she was married to her ex.

I had sympathy for Donna's father. After all, he was tortured in prison for seven years. Donna said he had wanted to kill himself in prison as some of his friends did, but because of Donna he didn't. Every time I saw him without a shirt, I wanted to see if there were scars of torture, yet I couldn't look.

Vinny's wedding wasn't like one I was expecting. The ceremony at "the boy's house" was only a few minutes and a few photos of eight huge trays of fruit, rice, and a giant cooked pig. The boy's family and friends then drove an hour to the girl's family's house to present her with the gifts. All the linens were red with gold tassels. There were embroidered designs of dragons, cartoon Asian faces, birds, and flowers, each brightly colored.

After an hour drive and waiting for every car to arrive at Connie's, especially the one with the pig, we could continue the ceremony. Connie wore a traditional Vietnamese headpiece that looked like a fabric crown that matched the garish pink of her dress with gold decoration. Vinny wore a bright yellow traditional outfit with the same gold decoration on the fabric. The ceremony was in a tight living room. Both Connie's parents walked her in. Donna's father presented Connie with gold jewelry. Each bridesmaid wore a different vividly colored dress, some Asian style, some American. There was a plethora of bright colors in the decorations, clothes, cups, and flowers, especially the color red. Even the food radiated color. The sticky rice was orange and the Jell-O molds were rainbow variations. The atmosphere looked like a Chinese New Year celebration.

Donna's dad held the microphone and he introduced each person in the family as they presented their gifts. He introduced Donna's ex as a brother-in-law, and then Donna and me as his daughter and a friend. Donna was disappointed, but I didn't expect more than that.

At the formal reception people brought their children and sat where they wanted, not assigned. The Asian restaurant had to bring more tables into the room. The planning seemed unorganized and created a stressful chaos you see in wedding movies. Vinny asked us to move twice. He thought my parents and I could sit by the other Americans, but there wasn't room for Donna. I felt he wasn't taking my relationship with Donna seriously or maybe he was embarrassed.

"I want to sit by Donna," I told him.

"She can pull up a chair," he said. His spiked hair with bleached tips stood off the top of his head like blades of grass. His muscular body was slightly visible under the tuxedo, which he had changed into.

"There are already ten places at the table, it's too tight to fit another one," I said.

"It's okay, honey, we'll find another place to sit," Donna said and left to look for one.

"Kel, it's okay, we can sit here," my mom said.

"No, I want to sit by you guys and Donna, I don't think that's too much to ask," I said, not letting Donna's brother tell us what to do, though it was his wedding. Donna reminded me she didn't want a Vietnamese wedding.

When my mother first walked in, I was surprised to see her without her wig. She wore an off-white hat with a blue flower pin in it. Her faded red and short thinning hair peeked out under her hat, another reminder she still had cancer. She said she wasn't going to dye her hair anymore.

Connie appeared in her white wedding gown, changing from her traditional colorful gown. The guests, who were almost all Vietnamese, took photos with her before she changed into a peach evening gown for the dance. Her high cheekbones were covered in a pink blush that matched the color above her eyes. Her black hair was lightened to a caramel brown. Connie's flamboyant, long nails were made conspicuous by their painted white tips; this display was expected as nails were her and Vinny's profession. Most of the female guests dressed up in dazzling colored and sparkly dresses.

In Vietnamese culture it's polite to ask the older generation to eat first. At the table Donna found for us, Mom and Tom were the oldest. The others at the table served them from the large plate of food. Chopsticks weren't foreign to my mother.

"So we get served first because we're older, huh?" Mom said amused by the new culture. Mom tried everything in the ten-course Asian meal, even the octopus. Donna smiled, impressed.

I glanced at Mom while she observed Donna's father giving a speech. His Parkinson's disease made his entire body shake. Donna's dad stood in his royal

50

blue traditional Vietnamese outfit. Silky and fitted, it closed at the shoulder like a Chinese gown. The shirt hung long below the waist and covered the top of his pants which could have passed for comfortable yet luxurious pajamas. His face looked stiff as his speech sounded like an order given to an army, though Donna's translation was the typical well wishes of a father to his son on his wedding day. Donna's other brother helped him back to his seat. When Mom and Tom were ready to leave we found Donna's parents and requested a photo. This was the first time our parents were together for a photo with us, and because of this my relationship with Donna felt more official. I smiled and enjoyed the idea of the contrast of cultures, colors, and generations juxtaposed in one image: my new family.

One night after Vinny's wedding, we visited Donna's family. In their culture, there's not much personal space. Everyone in the family will pile in one room and sit on one bed. I sat on Donna's parents' bed between Donna's mother and Kay's eight-year-old daughter. Donna's mother's jade necklace in the shape of Buddha sat heavy on her mother's chest.

"When you smile you are so pretty," I said to her mother in Vietnamese. "When Dad smiles he's handsome, but he never smiles," I said.

Donna's dad started to smirk and then stopped.

That night at dinner it was over 100 degrees in the house and they didn't turn on the air conditioning. Not used to the tropical feel of Vietnam that their place created, I drowned in my sweat. And of all food to eat on a hot day, it was roasted pig and pig intestines. On hot summer days my mother usually made salad or something cold to eat, not anything hot, and certainly never intestines.

The kids, or whoever couldn't fit at the small table, sat on the floor. I sat at the table. I had tried pig ears, chicken feet, duck liver, and goat, but I wasn't ready for intestines. Meat bones and chopsticks covered the table. After dinner I put a slice of orange in my mouth and kept the outer peel. I smiled creating a face with orange teeth. Donna's dad laughed.

Donna's niece gasped, excited, and said, "You made Grandpa laugh! No one can do that!"

I looked at this man whose stern face changed. I saw him differently. He did have a lighter side. Maybe he would come to our wedding and accept me as

51

a daughter-in-law. Either way, I was happy to be part of this family that was so different from mine, yet on some level, exactly the same.

Shoes

"You never really know a man until you stand in his shoes and walk around in them." –Harper Lee

The day I met Donna we weren't alone. Her friend, Lori, had been at the bar with her before I arrived. Lori felt the awkwardness of being a third wheel on a couple's first date. Luckily she didn't stay that long.

Ironically, Mom and Tom weren't alone on their first date either. I was their third wheel.

December 2002

It was the first Christmas after my father died and my mother and I had decided to take a New Year's ski vacation in Utah. Mom and I planned on driving and invited my boyfriend, Jimmy, to fly out and meet us. I had no idea my mother's relationship status was about to change again.

The day after Christmas we left for Utah. When Mom and I drove we always looked at the clouds and saw shapes. We both saw the same images. I could say, "That cloud looks like a person with a big nose," and Mom would know exactly which cloud.

My mother's long fingers moved over the tiny ring rosary as she held the steering wheel. Her fingernails were long and real, never fake. I could hear the sound of her lips moving while words of air spoke the silent prayers. Most of the time she drove there was no music and only occasional conversation between prayers. She liked the conversation, but then acted upset as if I interrupted her too many times, which I most likely did.

We stopped at a gas station. The previous Christmas I gave my mom a journal with questions about her and her life to answer like one I had given my dad. This Christmas Mom finished it and gave it back to me. She suggested I bring it with me and read it on our trip.

I read out loud the hopes I had written for both of us.

I hope we will maintain our close relationship if it can't get any closer, and that we'll live out our days together and enjoy my future kids.

I then read her hopes for me, which she wrote in her clean and consistent handwriting.

I hope we'll always be close and want to get together and do some traveling and that you never have to take care of me.

I looked at her and smiled, having read her words for the first time.

We hugged and cried at the gas station. I read on.

My greatest joy has been being a mother. I couldn't have made it without you, sweetheart! I could never love anyone else the way I love you--not even Dad.

I cried again. Love was painful, even when it felt good.

When we arrived at our second home in the Utah mountains after stopping for a night, the aftermath of the summer mess still existed. Last summer the heat unexpectedly came on (the outside temperature was over 100 degrees) and melted the candles, the butter in the fridge, and cracked and split the wood floor.

The builders hadn't fixed the floor and mouse droppings lay on our pillows. The water ran pink and foamy due to the heated driveway system backing up into our plumbing. And of course it was a Friday night so no one was available until Monday.

Then all of a sudden my mother's wrist started to hurt. I attributed it to clenching the steering wheel tightly while driving through the strong Wyoming wind. She started having something in between an anxiety attack and a temper tantrum.

"Mom, it's okay, we'll call the builder people's cell phone and see if we can get a hold of them; I'll get a warm washcloth for your arm, just take a breath."

"Don't tell me it's going to be okay. Don't tell me how to feel!"

I stood and stared at her in the kitchen as she grew younger in my mind, as young as a child.

"I'm only trying to help."

"You don't have to worry about anything. This is all my responsibility and Dad's not here to help me. Just leave me alone!" She looked away and grabbed the phone.

"Are you calling the builder?"

"Yes. Shit, answer your phone. Well, where's the washcloth?"

I brought her the washcloth without attitude and took a shower downstairs to get away. After my shower I walked up the steps to the kitchen to see her holding the phone.

"So, it's not a good idea to drink the water or shower in it?" she said to the phone.

I'm not supposed to shower in it? I just did. All the anxiety I held in burst out as tears. For some reason my mother thought that was funny. I liked seeing her laugh but it pissed me off when she laughed at me while I was crying. Her anger gradually waned as she talked to Aunt Giggly. I went downstairs to my room and found more mouse droppings.

Once Jimmy arrived, issues between my mother and me calmed down. It would have stayed that way had we not gone to the more advanced ski place the first day. Neither of us had skied in a year nor been to this particular ski resort for a few years. During the first ski run my mother thought she was going to die and put all the pressure on her thighs and complained the rest of the day.

The next day was far better than the previous, but tension was building. Jimmy was leaving in two more days. My mother and I would be alone again for the drive home. Mom agreed that we could take the scenic route home through the Grand Canyon, adding a few days to the drive. Had I known what those few days would entail, I would have given up the Grand Canyon in no time.

That evening I saw a flash of light out my window followed by a loud crackling. I opened the shades. From the mountain the view of the valley looked endless. All the streetlights sparkled like stars and Christmas lights flickered. The dark night filled with colored lights for miles. Then came another bright flash. Someone was setting off fireworks for New Year's. I could see some in the far distance from another suburb. Jimmy had already fallen asleep in the guest room. Happy New Year's, I said to myself.

The new year of 2003 brought with it a surprise.

"Can you find the house on this map?" Jimmy asked the next morning as he showed me a piece of paper with a map. Jimmy was tall with dark hair. His facial hair, never more than a few days old, sometimes displayed a small beard or side burns. His blue eyes, slightly crossed-eyed, had no depth perception unless he looked through binoculars. Like my dad, he grew up skinny with thick glasses, but now had contacts and worked out. Jimmy worked as a waiter and played trombone in a community band. His left deltoids muscle displayed a tattoo of an 8 ball and a 9 ball entwined.

"Yes. What's this?" I pointed to an address highlighted on the map.

"Ah, oh, that's where my uncle lives," he said to my surprise.

Of his mother's eleven siblings, all live in Minnesota except one, Tom, who happened to live in the exact city in Utah where my parents had bought a second home.

"Well, call him!" My mom said.

When Jimmy got a hold of Tom, he agreed to come skiing with us.

The entire day Tom and my mom never stopped exchanging stares. Later that evening out to dinner they kept exchanging bites of food. Jimmy and I looked at each other as if to say, "What kind of monsters did we create?"

Being the only sober one with depth perception, I drove Tom's car back to our house. Thank God Tom's car didn't have a stick shift because I couldn't drive one to save my life.

After Tom sobered up at our place he left, yet not without what looked like an awkward hug with my mother, the kind that lingers a little longer than it should.

The next morning Tom called to give my mother his "four other phone numbers," and she invited him over our last night there. We took Jimmy to the airport and packed for our road trip home.

At dinner that night, without Jimmy, I was the third wheel. I had been a third wheel before, but never on a date with my mother. I felt invisible. Neither of them made conversation with me. I stared at the metal fish sculptures on the wall while they flirted. After dinner they held hands as we walked to the car. I didn't even have a real brother to make me jealous of my mother's affection; this felt strange. I didn't know how to react.

I fell asleep before Tom left, and when I awoke in the morning my mother confessed he hadn't left till 3am. Since I had slept more than Mom I started out driving. My mother, unfortunately not fast asleep, sank easily into her usual role of backseat driver.

"Get in the right lane. The left lane's only for passing. Slow down. Pass that truck. Get back in the right lane! Stay in the right lane except to pass!"

I had heard enough. "Fine!"

56

Trying to drive with constant, mostly unnecessary criticism is strenuous and particularly impossible to tune out when it's your mother. I clenched my teeth like someone else's two-year-old was screaming in my ear.

"We're not even going to make it to Arizona tonight and it's starting to get dark. I'm tired." Her voice went from a complaining adult to a whining child.

"It's not my fault you stayed up till three in the morning."

The conversation ended for a while and we spent the night in southern Utah at the entrance to Zion National Park. My mother complained while driving through it the next day.

"Yes, it's beautiful. Slow down, the road might be slippery. Oh God, I hate the edge. Speed up going up this hill. Stay on your side!"

How could I see the beauty of the park when every thought became about what I was doing wrong? I felt like I was maneuvering a driving course and she was my guide, or rather my drill sergeant.

We made it as far as chilly Flagstaff that night. As someone from Minnesota, a state most others assume is always cold, I thought Arizona was supposed to be warm. I sat on the bed writing a postcard to a friend, surprised when I realized what I just wrote. I had written my mother's first name down instead of "Mom."

Who was this woman I had known my whole life but was now acting like a stranger? Who was this woman who, as a girl, played in lilac bushes, whom now I wanted to picture running in thorns? Who never went without a perm? Who gave my father ten minutes to pick my middle name? Who baked cakes and frosting almost every day for people's birthdays, weddings, and piano recitals? Sometimes she still smelled like the sweetness of the frosting. I smelled it now. The cocoa in the chocolate mixture. The marble swirl of cake batter. The leftover pie crust baking in the oven with butter and cinnamon sugar on it for us to share.

But then the sound of the sewing machine hissed in my memory. It started out steady and smooth like a dial tone and then became louder and fierce. Then the sound of the Serger, like a wood chipper. The sound of the chair rolling over linoleum and the quick cut of the scissors on thread, the chair rolling back, only to have the needle pierce the fabric again.

"My hair looks terrible," she said, piercing my memory. "This curling iron isn't working. I hate this bathroom. My hair looks terrible. I need to get another curling iron. We'll go to a Walmart. I didn't see one on the way here. I hate my hair. I need better shampoo, this hotel shampoo is shit."

I looked at my mother for the first time in a while; she rarely swore. Mom's blue eyes appeared aqua in the light. Her pearl clip-on earrings hid behind her hair that sat a few inches above her shoulders. Terrified of needles, she had never pierced her ears or gotten a tattoo.

Our second visit to Walmart on the trip semi-satisfied her. Exhausted from the complaining, I slept well that night.

The next day it rained. Freezing rain. Whenever it rained at home my mother turned on the news, grabbed the flashlight with extra batteries, put on her tennis shoes, and took the cats to the basement with her. This ritual occurred throughout my life. One night, while my mother and I were "camping" under the stairs, I asked her, "Why is Daddy still upstairs in bed?" She answered, "He believes in probability. I'd rather be safe than sorry."

At age 14, my mother experienced the largest tornado outbreak in Minnesota. It was voted the "fifth most significant Minnesota Weather Event of the 20th Century" by the Minnesota Climatology Office. Six tornados had gone through Minnesota the evening of May 6th, 1965. The two largest, F-4s, some still debate were F-5s, had damaged my mother's neighborhood. Her father had gone to get milk at the strip mall after the first storm had gone through. He came back to the house without milk. "Where's the milk?" the family asked. "The mall is gone," he said. Then they piled in the basement with some neighbors while the tornado from the second storm system damaged the high school gym and their neighborhood.

After the storm my mom's family walked upstairs and cut their bare feet on broken glass; they hadn't thought to bring their shoes downstairs. Their clothes, scattered everywhere, were covered in black oil from some chemical plant in the area. A huge piece of wood came through the wall and into the crib where my mother's youngest brother slept moments before. The brand new swing-set my grandpa had bought and laid out on the lawn to be assembled was gone. My grandpa walked outside and said, "I guess I don't have to clean out the garage now." Their garage was on top of their neighbor's home four houses down the block. I understood my mother's fears...and perhaps that explained my reoccurring nightmare of tornadoes.

Mom gave me ten minutes to get out of the car and look at the Grand Canyon. Seeing this spectacular site for the first time, the 40 shades of brown earth dividing one side and the other, didn't look or feel as grand on this cloudy day surrounded by snow and bitterness. What was once divided by a river now stood dry and desolate like the space between my mother and me.

We left the snow in Arizona but took the tension all the way to Texas. New Mexico may have looked prettier had I been in a better mood to enjoy it. Oklahoma was flat, uninteresting, and didn't show me any sympathy.

Finally, we made it to Texas, which was ironically colder than Minnesota. I decided I hated January, or maybe only the northern hemisphere. And most of all, I now hated anywhere my mother was.

We sat, emotionally and physically exhausted, in a Mexican restaurant in Texas, despising each other and talking out the animosity that had been building up for days.

The three main things that make me cry are: death of a loved one, being completely stressed out, and my mother yelling at me. Now all those things at the same time made me cry in this restaurant. I'm not the kind of person who cries in front of anyone but my mother, let alone in a public place. I almost smiled, remembering my mother hated Mexican food. But no smile could break through this anger.

"If you complain about one more thing, I think I might go insane!" I said in the calmest voice I could muster.

"I just want to go home."

"Mom, we can't worry about that now, we'll drive home tomorrow." I stared at the table.

"Don't tell me what I can worry about!"

"Do you want me to drive you to the airport and I'll just drive home?" I said in a serious voice.

Silence. We both knew that idea wasn't practical, though I pictured it happening.

The bright colors of yellow and green painted on the walls and paintings of red flowers failed at cheering me up. Our poor waiter now saw my tears. I asked him in a surprisingly composed voice for more napkins without taking my eyes off the table. He brought about fifty.

"Mom, it just shouldn't be this hard." My exhaustion made my voice calm.

"What do you mean it shouldn't be this hard?!" She started to become more hysterical.

"Mom, you aren't even being tolerable."

"I don't know why I let us do this. I'm not a road trip person," she said to the table.

"I'm sorry," I said, feeling guilty.

"You can go on road trips with your friends. I won't ever do this again."

"Mom it's fine. It's only one more night."

"Don't tell me everything's fine. I have the right to feel."

I looked up to see if her eyes were wet. They were dry.

"Mom, it's so hard when everything that comes out of your mouth is negative."

"Well you can't just brush it off and tell me I can't have feelings. You've been doing that all the time!"

I pretended to look for a response in my food.

"Well maybe it's the only way I can react to it!" I said, "I'm sorry that Dad's not here to travel with and help figure things out, but I'm trying to help."

"I thought I'd do this for you. Ah, I guess that wasn't a good idea." Finally she was calming down, maybe because I mentioned Dad.

"I guess it wasn't. I don't think we were thinking clearly. Maybe you need to think about yourself sometimes," I said nicely.

"Well, you're such a kid! You get into that kid role!"

"I can't help getting into that role. You're still my mother and I'm always going to be your daughter. I try to be responsible. I looked up all the information and planned this trip. I'm trying not to be the kid when I'm with you but sometimes I can't help it. I'm trying! Can you give me an example then of when I was acting like a kid so I can work on it?"

"Well, just forget it. Never mind. I guess it'll always be like that." She looked down at her plate.

"There are too many issues and too many things going on and we are both emotionally exhausted. I don't think we can talk about it anymore," I said.

"You're right. There are too many issues." She looked up at the waiter. "I'll take the check now please, thanks."

Winning against your mother is like overthrowing the government, a *coup d'état*. But in the end the satisfaction of winning the battle isn't worth the ruins and casualties and disorder you're left with.

Later that night Mom lingered in the bathroom talking to Tom on her cell while I watched *ER*.

"These batteries are supposed to last longer!" she said when she came out of the bathroom and threw the cell phone on the bed.

"How's Tom?"

"Good," she said sweetly, like the cliché of a young girl in love.

Tom was about the only thing we could talk about that lightened the mood, if only for a few minutes.

We drove straight up I-35 the next day. My mother is someone who can't spend a night in a hotel if she's only a state away from home. We were four.

"We're driving all the way home tonight; we should be home before 11."

"Fine."

"You can lean your seat back."

"Okay."

Both exhausted, we found lighter subjects to talk about. Mom listened to her CDs, which I preferred over silent prayers. It was to be a smooth last couple hundred miles, or so I thought.

"What was that?" I said to a beeping noise.

"Shit! We're almost out of gas!"

"Mom, it's okay, don't panic."

"Don't tell me that! Oh my God, I forgot to fill up last time. I don't know if there's a gas station!"

"Mom, when the light comes on we still have about 30 miles we can drive. I saw the special they did on TV about when you'll actually run out of gas."

"Pisshead! Is that a sign, what does it say?!"

My mother hated when the tank went under a half and now it blinked empty. She also hated getting off the freeway when she couldn't see where to get back on. Of course the exit we chose took us far away from the freeway.

"How far away is this goddamned gas station! There's no sign, I don't even know where to go!"

"Mom, it's okay. Calm down. It looks like it's up there."

Thank God I saw something resembling a station.

"You don't know it's going to be okay. Stop dismissing my feelings! It's seven below outside! We need gas! Shit, it doesn't have a credit card thing!"

"Yes it does. Do you want me to do it?"

"Why?"

"Because I haven't put gas in yet, and it's cold out."

She got out and the credit card machine didn't work, and the inside looked closed.

"Shit shit shit! What are we gonna do?"

"We'll get back on the freeway and go to the next exit. Mom, don't worry. We'll find a gas station."

"Just shut up. You don't know there's a gas station! Shit!"

I always hear that there comes a time in a woman's life when she sees her mother as a person and not just a mother. I thought I had experienced that occasionally in the last few years, but this time I really understood what it meant. I witnessed what I thought to be my mother's weakest moment. My father could have calmed her down and taken some of the responsibility; she never let me take any. I kept my mouth shut. There wasn't one word I could say that would help. I shut down like a computer. I put on my headphones and turned up my music and closed my eyes tightly. I had no control over anything but myself. My mother, blinded by her anger and panic, lost control.

"Stupid, stupid, I can't believe I did that!" At least she didn't blame that one on me.

We found another gas station and made it home by midnight. I slept over and drove home to my place the next day. We parted with no eye contact and a stoic "I love you" and didn't talk for a week.

Two weeks later Mom called the doctor on the way to pick up Tom from the airport. "Breast cancer," the doctor told her.

Now she was the one in my father's shoes. The one people felt sorry for, the one people were afraid to call, the one fighting to live.

*

Donna wouldn't let me have shoes with heels for the wedding because it would make her look even shorter. "People will think you're marrying a midget or I'm marrying a giant," she said.

Donna was already over seven inches shorter than me. Therefore, I decided to get comfy yet stylish flip-flops. I searched several stores until I found a comfortable and affordable pair; white with silver sparkly jewels. A contemporary, gay Cinderella look.

Photos

Finding a wedding photographer who's affordable but experienced isn't easy. Donna and I decided to chance it on a photographer a friend recommended.

The last time I had been in front of a professional photographer was the weekend before Momtom got married. It was 2005 and Tom's kids were in town so Mom wanted a professional family portrait taken. I sat with them and looked at the camera, feeling strange. I had only seen my step siblings fewer than ten times, maybe fewer than five. The three sisters had each other and two of them had children. I smiled for the pictures like a recently adopted foreign child.

But a portrait or photo can't capture the story of fear or pain. The film only gets to see what the shutter allows it to. And the longer the shutter is open the more exposed the film is, letting in too much light, causing the film to go black.

February 2003

When I was still in art college, my mother asked me to draw her nude portrait before her body became different from a lumpectomy. Taking showers with her as a child and having drawn her previously for drawing assignments, my eyes were used to her body. While she lay on the chaise lounge the fear of change hid on her face. I sat in my mother's living room remembering what my Watercolor professor had told us in class the week before. "Don't worry about painting what you see, but paint the essence of it," the professor said. I tried to capture my mother's distilled spirit, her essence. I looked down at the dark gray charcoal shards that sullied my fingers. How do I capture this essence of my mother? The essence of my mother was more than her body. Her body would change, but her essence would not. Her powerful presence could crush a room, but not in a destructive way. The way a child's pillow fort falls to the ground and covers you with its softness. I picked up my white eraser, now gray with the black ashes of my medium. Will anything keep her close when her essence is gone?

Goldfish were flushed and forgotten.

The previous week my Watercolor professor had dropped one of the bags of goldfish we were painting. Trying to save them, he quickly filled the bag with water from the sink in the painting room. Minneapolis city water filled their lungs like smoke.

I sat down at one of the small tables in the room with the tall ceiling. Natural light came through the room-sized studio windows. I got my supplies ready as did the other twelve students. The bag of goldfish rested on the table in front of me. One of the three goldfish had risen to the top and now floated upside-down. I wanted to cry. Why was I falling apart this easily, especially at school during class? I wanted to leave the classroom, but if I did I was sure I would cry. What would I tell the professor? That I felt bad for a fish? That my father had been a goldfish in faucet water gradually swimming slower and floating to the surface? That my mother was that goldfish, too, and was thrown back in the distilled water with the others, but maybe not soon enough?

Goldfish die faster in faucet water than distilled.

During the painting session the second goldfish slowly rose to the surface of the bag. Why did *our* table have to get the bag of death? Was it a stigma that now followed me?

The other students kept on painting, not seeing my agony. I looked down at my paper. The ultramarine blue choked the cadmium orange of the goldfish to the edge of the composition. The technique known as "wet on wet" only looked like a polluted puddle. Water from my brush drowned the Cold Press watercolor paper.

"Two are dead!" yelled the skinny girl at my table with the flower-patterned shirt.

I wanted her to cry so that I could cry with her.

My family sat before me, encased in a bag. I swam in a suffocating bag of contaminated water moving slower and slower. I watched my lifeless parents rise to the top, anticipating the moment when I also would no longer breathe. At least a goldfish's memory only lasts two minutes. Reminders of my orphan nightmare never stopped.

Goldfish die faster in faucet water than distilled.

Tears. I stopped painting. So did the skinny girl.

"I'm puttin' the live one in the bag with the ones in the distilled water," she said as she got up and did it not waiting for approval.

Finally an angel! I was saved! Though a parentless child, I could go on living in life-breathing water again.

"Don't worry about painting what you see, but paint the essence of it," the professor said.

*

I looked through some photos of Dad to put out at our wedding ceremony. As I was looking through my drawer I found the papers with questions on them I asked my dad. He had answered all of them before he died. I sat down and read some. Then I knew how my dad would still be able to be at my wedding. I had asked him to write down advice for my future spouse. I could read it at the wedding and it would be like he was giving a toast and his advice. He would be there in his words, in his spirit, and in his photos.

His advice for my future spouse:

Listen to your wife. Respect her feelings. If you get very angry, stop and cool off and resume the conversation later. Set periodic times to do fun things together. Things change and interests change- try to experience new hobbies and interests together. Try to understand each other and where the other person is coming from. Understand your wife's needs, wants and desires. Try lots of little things to make your wife happy. Be open and honest and communicate as often as possible. Eat celery with peanut butter.

Hair

I had a dream I lost my hair. It came out in chunks and in its place were spider bites that turned red and grew into anthills.

<u>March 2003</u>

I remember sitting with my mother outside on the bench in front of her house. It was May or June. Either Dad was sick in bed or well in Heaven, but it was just her and me. After a long pause she said, "It's the temperature of Heaven."

It was the air in which worries float away. It was the one moment of peace everyone expects yet rarely finds. We had it together.

That memory came back to me as I sat in the hospital waiting room waiting for them to prep my mother before her lumpectomy. I tried to keep the thought of losing her out of my mind. My dad hadn't been gone for a year yet, and I had to deal with the idea of losing another parent. My mother acted so strong on the outside that it was easy to overlook her own loss of health and physical perception.

When the team of nurses finished prepping my mother for surgery they let us visit her. The room was bright with white lights, white walls, and a white bed with a white blanket. The room resembled an artist's bleached canvas, but not one that invited color and creativity, one that covered it up.

Mom didn't look scared like I had expected. She looked peaceful and calm. I held her hand as she lay in the hospital bed. Her sisters and brother walked back to the waiting room, leaving us alone.

"I'm going to get through this for you and Tom," she said.

She looked down at our hands and then back at me as her eyes started to water.

"I'm okay, Mom, really."

"I'm proud you're my brave daughter," she said, looking at me, squeezing my hand.

I sat in the crowded waiting room with my aunts and uncles. I attempted to read <u>The Hours</u> by Michael Cunningham, while the surgeon removed the cancer from my mother's breast, the one that covered her heart. An hour or two later the surgeon appeared.

"She's in recovery, everything went well. Ah, we did find that the cancer had spread to the main lymph node and two others of the thirteen we removed. I really feel that we got it all, but the pathology report on Monday will tell for sure."

We sat back down in the chairs and my mother's closest sister, Aunt Giggly, explained the news to the ones who couldn't hear what the surgeon had said.

Then I lost it. I hadn't really cried about her cancer yet. Tears flowed but no sobs. Aunt Giggly held me to her breast and I hid my face under her arm against her dark green shirt. I didn't want to pull away. I stayed there until I felt composure returning.

It was good news. Good news. The surgeon said so. He thinks they got it all. She's fine. She's in recovery. My dad's brother had died in recovery from a blood clot. I cried again.

I couldn't get the word "spread" out of my brain. Spreading meant it could go everywhere. My father's cancer spread from the pancreas to the liver. We found it in the last stage. My mother's was found in stage two. With breast cancer you could still be saved in the first part of stage four. But it had spread. How could this surgery save my mother from cancer, yet there hadn't been a surgery to save my father? It didn't make sense to me. I was only familiar with the kind of cancer that took your life in fewer than seven months. This cancer didn't do that? I didn't understand.

My mother's three younger sisters, Aunt Giggly, Aunt Quiet, and Aunt Stubborn, followed me to the recovery room. They all acted calm and quiet; perhaps trying to be strong. My mother looked pale and her thin hair lie slicked back. So relieved to see her alive, I didn't notice she looked ten years older.

Mom requested some oxygen and the nurse appeared.

"Are these your daughters?" the nurse asked.

We looked at each other tensely.

"I'm the daughter," I said quickly, hoping my mother didn't pick up on the unfavorable reference to her age. Her eyes were closed as she rested.

"Do you think she heard that?" Aunt Stubborn whispered.

"Yes I did!" my mother said in a loud angry voice that made us jump.

We smiled, relieved she was more alive than she looked.

Mom was able to come home and I stayed at her house with her. The pathology report came an annoying day late.

"I don't care. Postponing what could be bad news is fine," my mother said. But I knew her better; she hated waiting.

To pass the time I looked at my mom's collection of books from my childhood. I grabbed Sleeping Beauty off the shelf. It was illustrated with photographs of dolls. The witch had scared me so badly when I was little I had taken crayons and tried to color over her. Fear can't be colored or painted over. You have to look it right in the face until it doesn't scare you anymore.

The next day brought the good news we hoped for. They got it all. Yet there was always a *but*: they felt she needed to have chemo before her radiation to flush out her system of any cancer cells left floating around. Having watched my father go through chemo, Mom was definitely not looking forward to it.

The idea of the chemo acting as a precaution instead of attempting to be a cure sounded better. Yet there was still the worry of her immune system being weak and her catching a cold. And then comes the visual change, the bald look that screams chemo.

"I've always hated my hair," Mom told me. "I want to lose it. Maybe it will come back curly like they say it does. I'm going to pick out wigs." I admired her for finding a little joy in the hard change cancer forced her to go through.

A week later my mother stopped by on her way to the airport to pick up Tom. She wanted to show me her wig. My friend Alice had come to visit for the day. My two-bedroom condo wasn't as clean as my mother would have it. The walls weren't white or tan; they were covered with my murals of clouds and butterflies. Junk I needed to take upstairs occupied three steps.

I opened the door for my mother. She stepped inside. She looked like a relative of ours; I couldn't say which one. Her face was familiar but her hair was not. The wig, a dark red, stood out in contrast to my faded auburn color. A barrette held the sides of the hair and the bangs that rested just above her eyebrows.

We looked like twins. My mother looked younger and made me look older.

"You look like the daughter and you look like the mother," Alice said bluntly.

My mother even acted younger. I noticed we had the same tone of voice and same expressions. She giggled like a girl and wore her new boot cut jeans over high-heeled caramel-colored boots. She sat at my kitchen table and painted her fingernails the shade of her wig, smiling and laughing between bits of conversation.

"She has eyes in the back of her head," I said to Alice in our conversation about my mother.

"I don't anymore. My wig covers them up." My mother joked as if humor now came easily to her.

Once we accepted a situation, my mother and I tried to see the humor in it.

I looked at my mother noticing her beauty. The Rosacea on her cheeks was less discernable. She wore eye make-up and lipstick only on special occasions. Since Tom came along her confidence made her beauty shine.

When I closed the door after my mother left, Alice said, "It was like there were two of you."

I had noticed it also. My mother was like me. With the same look of possibility in her eyes, she now looked like me. She felt young and giddy. She was a girl with a new hairdo who painted her nails and fit into her sexy jeans going to pick up her boyfriend at the airport. This was not the mother I knew. But she was happy despite the cancer.

I wondered what it would be like to have seen my mother at my age. I also wondered what it would be like to see yourself outside of yourself. This was the closest I would ever get.

A memory came to me. I remembered when my mother and I met up with Jimmy at a gas station and he came late.

"Let's go walk up the street and stand on the corner with a sign and wave," my mom said.

"That would be hilarious! Let's do it," I said, half joking, thinking my mother was kidding.

"Come on," she said.

"Really?" I couldn't believe she was serious.

I grabbed a pen and paper from the gas station and made a welcome sign and we started walking up the street. "It's not like you to do something like this, Mom."

"You don't know me very well."

How could she say I didn't know her? I had known her my whole life. She told me about everything. I thought I knew her pretty well. Did she do this to show me that she could be cool and stand on street corners with signs like a teenager? What was it about her I didn't know?

Now I knew I didn't really know her. I knew my mother as a mother. I recently got to know her as a widow and single woman who became "the girlfriend of my boyfriend's uncle." I didn't know her as young. Now I did. She had the spunk put back in her that life had taken away throughout the years.

I wasn't ready to be optimistic about the whole idea of her spunkiness and bliss. What goes up must come down, and with the chemo treatments starting the next week she would be exhausted, sick, and crabby. Menopause was bad enough, but mixing it with chemo…who knew?

My mother married her first husband, Jay, at 19 who never looked my grandmother in the eye. He went a little crazy and pushed my mother once. One day he ended up in a mental hospital.

"Jay may never recover from his illness," the doctor told my mom. "You're so young. You may want to consider leaving him."

She handed the doctor some photos.

"This makes a lot of sense now in his case," the doctor told her.

They were photos of Jay dressed in women's clothing. My mom originally thought it was just for fun. Until one day she came home and saw he had bought her an outfit of a skirt and Gogo boots. She looked in his closet and saw he had bought the same thing for himself in his size. She left Jay in the hospital and divorced him at nineteen, a marriage of six months.

Her second husband became just a friend and roommate who didn't want kids.

My mother knew it was true love when she met my father. She told me, "When you know, you know." They were together "'til death do us part."

Mom said she didn't want anyone after my father died. She hadn't been looking for anyone, but then she met Tom, this young man with a full head of hair and a soft voice. This Catholic, 42-year-old grandpa had been surrounded by women his whole life. Tom grew up with nine sisters and two brothers, married the woman he got pregnant at seventeen, and had three daughters and two granddaughters.

When my mother started dating again, I worried. I wasn't worried about her getting her heart broken by a breakup; I was worried she could lose another husband to cancer. Ironically now she was the one with cancer.

Mom wasn't supposed to drive because she had a port put in for her Chemo treatments starting this week. When Mom asked me to drive Tom back to the airport, it was the last thing I wanted to do. Yet my mother needed me and I would follow through.

"Grandpa and Grandma would love to," she said, still in a voice that made me feel guilty if I said no.

"No, it's okay, I'll do it."

"Tom made sloppy-joes."

"I don't like sloppy-joes," I said like a child.

"But these are different," my mother said, defending him. I knew she could tell my attitude from my statement.

I ate the sloppy-joes anyway; they actually weren't that bad. I passed by opportunities to make sarcastic comments to Tom. I was crabby and chose not to say anything. That didn't work. Mom could see right through me like she always could.

I felt the jealous daughter in me as I watched my mother hug her boyfriend as he left for his plane. Tom made a joke. She laughed, saying it hurt her neck when she laughed. The tape held on the gauze above the metal port beneath her skin.

"Maybe you didn't think my operation today was a big deal," she said when we got back in the car, "but it was for me."

"Well I'm glad Tom was there for you. I haven't been in your life much."

"No, you haven't, and I know you have a lot to do, but being crabby right now is not the best thing. I don't have time to deal with trivial stuff anymore."

"I have a lot on my mind."

"Then why don't you get rid of some. You are going skiing this weekend and then that trip with your friends over spring break. You'll have plenty of time for fun then. Stop trying to make time for things you want to do now, only do the things you have to do. Is school stuff going okay?"

I thought about this weekend skiing, being in Utah for the first time without her. Only Tom, Jimmy, and me. No rules. I could be free and not worry that I didn't make the bed right or forget to put my bowl in the sink.

"I guess."

"You guess."

"Just leave me to deal with it. I need to process everything, I'll be fine." I bit my lip, trying to stop tears.

I wanted to make her laugh so her neck would hurt. I wanted her to feel the misery I felt. These were the last days of my mother before she started Chemo for the next twenty-five weeks. My own worries were piling up and people were asking me to do things. I was sick of the world. I wanted to go on a ship by myself for a few months and sit there and watch the ocean pass by.

I hated the phone calls I received. Someone would be sad about his or her uncle's neighbor's dog dying. I couldn't even conjure up fake sympathy. My father's dead and my mom's sick and I'm supposed to care about someone's dog they barely knew? I hated people saying on the phone, "Oh, this must be such a hard time," yet I hated it more when people wouldn't acknowledge it at all.

Either way it didn't matter. I was alone in my torment. I almost liked it. I could be as selfish as I wanted, but then it came back to my mother and what she needed and how her misery was worse than mine. I should be thinking about her at a time like this and if I didn't I was a terrible person. I needed a mother's comfort to ease my pain, but how could I ask for it from the one who was hurting?

The more Momtom were together, the more alone I felt, though sometimes I'd feel like we were a family because there were three of us. But then I'd be the child again, the only child, alone with her thoughts dissolving into the back seat of the car while nobody noticed. A world lived inside my head that nobody knew. I could put people there and take them away, make-up new people and anything I wanted to happen would happen. Yet it was a child's game. But, like a child, I cried easily now.

"I think maybe you're a little upset about Tom," Mom said when we arrived home.

"No, it's not him," I said. "It's nothing, I just haven't processed the work I have to get done, that's all. Where's my stuff?" I opened my drawer looking for my toothbrush.

"I moved your stuff to the bottom drawer."

My toiletries had been demoted to the bottom drawer now that Tom used the bathroom, too. I only used her bathroom when I stayed to keep her company when she got ready for bed. Mom liked having someone there to race while she got ready. She hated it when Dad would be in bed before her with his teeth brushed.

I left the room.

My mother didn't need this crying mess of a daughter on top of everything. The fantasy of traveling with my mother to foreign countries, our bond becoming stronger until we couldn't stand each other for another moment, faded away because of her new companion. There's a reason why the seasons don't change in a day. Was I jealous? I wanted her to be happy. But I was jealous.

The next day she told me Tom had decided to quit his job and move back to Minnesota to help her through her chemo treatments. The happiness was back in her voice, but I realized we wouldn't have much time alone anymore before the chemo and before Tom moved in.

The black case I used to sit in as a baby housed my dad's guitar. I opened it. It smelled the same: musty, metallic, like a cold garage.

I played for a while then chatted with Mom as she opened mail in bed. I took care of her like she had once taken care of dad, making her dinner and cleaning the cats' litter box.

I hated doing dishes. Washing dishes was always my punishment as a child. It wasn't the actual act, but the idea of doing them I hated. One time my mother tried to convince my father and me that we didn't love her because we didn't occasionally wash dishes for her.

"Don't you know how the plates go in the rack?" she asked, coming into the kitchen to help.

"Yes. I just didn't think it mattered."

"It does if you want them to drip-dry," Mom said. She still critiqued the way I did dishes. Tonight I did her dishes because I loved her. I finally understood what it meant to do dishes for someone because of love.

While I dealt with feeling like an orphan, my mother dealt with symptoms. She used cream in her nose. She lost her nose hairs to chemo and sores developed inside her nostrils. She also lost the protection of her eyelashes covering her eyes. It reminded her of when she was young and her elbow slipped off the counter and the eyelash curler pulled out every eyelash.

For Thanksgiving 2004, we went to Tom's sister's house. Among Tom's eleven siblings, I was the only stepchild. The twenty-two cousins grew up together, making me feel like a stranger. And, of course, my ex-boyfriend Jimmy was one of the cousins. Jimmy and I were still friends but it was his family, not mine. We had broken up because I didn't want to have sex before marriage and he thought I wouldn't ever want to. Years later I realized that it wasn't me not wanting to have sex before marriage, but me not wanting to have sex with a guy.

I tried to be outgoing and chat with Tom's sisters. Mom told me later, "You help me fit into Tom's family."

Of Tom's nine sisters my favorite was Maggie. Petite with tan skin and dark hair, Maggie, an artist, was strong, single, and wild. She would say anything to get a reaction and she swore a lot. Maggie got cancer a couple years later. They removed her arm and her shoulder before it consumed her, and she died at 42 years old.

Before Maggie died I entered an art show with her that dealt with cancer. When my mother lost her hair to chemo, she bought various hats and wigs to cover her bald head. I noticed how her personality changed from wig to wig and hat to hat. For a class in college, I created a series of watercolor portraits of my mother in each hat and wig, and the emotion or personality each conveyed. The painting that was the most successful I submitted to the show. It portrayed my mother in a melancholy, reflective state, though the overall emotion she exhibited throughout her recovery was bravery.

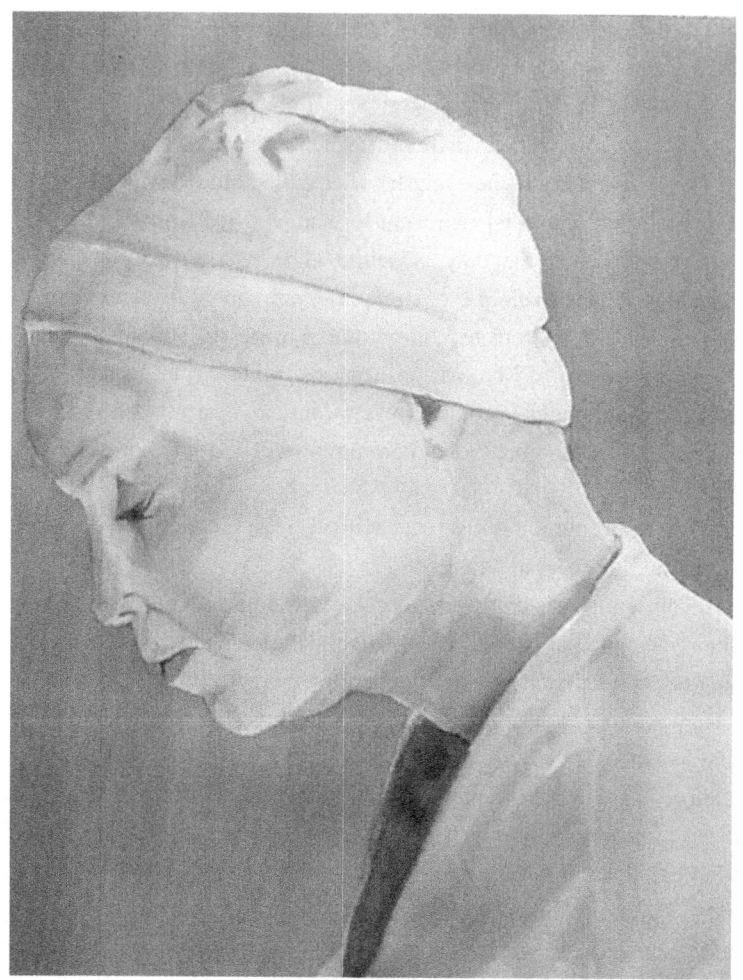

Frankenberg, Kelly. <u>Untitled Number 5</u>. 2003.

It took till December that year, nearly a year after Mom's surgery, before she felt better and her hair grew back.

*

By 2012, my dyed long reddish brown hair was down to the center of my back. My friend from high school said she would fix our hair for the wedding. I looked at a photo on my bookshelf. It was from the last trip Mom and Dad and I took together before Dad got sick. My hair was long with curls and a flower was pinned on the side. That's how I wanted my hair.

Flowers

Different colored orchids, birds of paradise, bamboo, thick green leaves, hibiscus, and passionflowers bloomed in my brain. I wanted Hawaiian flowers for the wedding. My mother had lived in Hawaii in the 70s with her second husband. Eventually they moved back to the mainland because paradise sadly became too much work, and without enough money, no fun. Hawaii, however, was still Mom's favorite vacation destination.

To save money, I set out to make my own bouquets for the ceremony. Color was important. Who said you can't have irises with birds of paradise?

As I looked through the options of flowers, a memory came to me from my teen years: picking flowers on a mountain in Norway. It was another time in my life I tried to be happy when my mother was sick.

July 1995

I had woken up in a dark hotel room in Lillehammer; bright yellow light entered from behind the curtain. My mother lay in the bed next to me.

"I have a fever," she said in a raspy voice, "but I'll be fine. I just need to stay in bed."

I told the hotel desk she was sick and asked if they could bring her some tea and crackers and not disturb her.

Leaving the hotel, I felt free for the first time in my life. I was 14, had finished school for the summer, and was no longer under my mother's watch. The sunlight followed me as I walked down the street. You'd never have known this main street, surprisingly minute and calm, had seen millions when it hosted the Olympics eighteen months ago. Locals and tourists came in and out of shops in no hurry. American music played on the street corners and Olympic souvenirs still hung in shops. Almost everyone spoke English.

I walked with confidence the few blocks to the gate that led up to our relative's home right on the main street. We had been there the previous night, so I knew where it was. I stepped up the tiny dirt hill to see the young boys outside running around. They were about two and five with pale skin that looked orange in the sun. Their white-blonde hair was long enough to cause them to be mistaken for girls, but their nudity answered the question.

78

"Good morning," Ingrid said as she appeared at the door.

Ingrid stood tall with long carelessly uncombed black hair. Despite her blue eyes she looked plain, but that's what made her so beautiful. The veins in her arms popped out slightly more than usual; maybe from the days she played drums in an all-girl band.

"My mom's sick; she won't be able to come," I told her. I loved knowing I was experiencing this adventure on my own.

"I taught ve'd pick some vild flewers fur da funeral," Ingrid said.

"Sure, that sounds fun."

We got in the car. It was a stick shift. I sat in the passenger seat.

"Vant to try?" Ingrid asked, explaining how to put the car into gear. Unsure, I grabbed the lever.

"I think it's in reverse," I said.

"Ve'll see," she said and stepped on the gas.

We drove straight forward into the wooden fence.

I smiled with embarrassment.

"Tat's okay," she said.

Ingrid drove us up into the mountains covered with grass and wildflowers. I looked at my legs, embarrassed because I hadn't shaved in a while. Then I noticed hers. She never shaved a day in her life. I fantasized about living in the mountains, not shaving, raising little boys who grew their hair long and ran around naked whenever they pleased.

We passed cows.

"Jacob, what does a cow say?" Ingrid asked in Norwegian.

"Moo!" Jacob said. His older brother echoed.

I understood what Ingrid had asked based on the response. I smiled, expecting a cow to speak differently because it was a different country.

Ingrid stopped the car so I could see the Olympic ski jumps from this distance. We then drove onto a tiny road where Ingrid told me the healer lived. We picked the most beautiful wild flowers, the kind you could only buy at a flower shop in America.

"I tink Signe vill like dees," Ingrid said.

The boys danced around, this time with their clothes on.

My family had visited Signe the year before she passed away. I didn't know why we had come back for the funeral. Probably because my mother never missed out on a funeral for a distant relative, though this was the first funeral overseas.

From the time I understood death I attended more funerals than I could count. One funeral in particular stood out in my memory (aside from the one where a fly landed on my cousin's nose and I burst out laughing). It was the funeral for my great aunt's mother.

My great aunt's mother had an artificial leg. Someone always put me on her lap for a photo when I was a child. I hated it because her fake leg terrified me. At the funeral my great aunt cried so loudly the room shook. At eight years old, with twenty funerals of experience, I never heard an adult sob so loud. At that time I realized no matter what age, losing my mother would be excruciating.

Ingrid took me by a waterfall. I sat down. The powerful beauty of the water made me feel like I might fall over. Light green grass filled in around it. The pure air made moss grow on the rocks and trees. The water rushed softly, entering a small pool below. The pool encased shards of sun and reflected brilliant greens and blues. I sat and worshiped it as if it were a god, promising myself I would come back and paint it before I died.

My high from the morning remained when my grandparents arrived at Ingrid's for the funeral. My mother's parents had traveled with us. Dad had to work and he usually preferred to stay home, especially when it was traveling for a funeral.

Ingrid's husband Aksel stepped out of the house to greet me. Aksel was a thin man, barely taller than Ingrid. His light brown hair hinted that he used to be blonde as a kid. His crooked smile welcomed me like a comforting hug.

I sat by my grandparents and Ingrid at the funeral service. I hadn't thought the funeral would be in Norwegian. I barely recognized when they said her name. As the casket was lowered into the hole in the ground, we placed the wildflowers, now wilting, on top.

Back at Ingrid's, my grandparents stayed and chatted with her and some others while Aksel took the boys and me swimming. I hadn't brought a swimsuit, so I wore some shorts and my black sports bra. Embarrassed because it wasn't really a swimsuit, I wore a shirt over it while we walked up the hill.

We hiked up a trail surrounded by pine trees and passed only one party of tourists. Then it was only us and nature. We stopped at a point on the trail and then stepped down the rocks to the water. Aksel stepped in first and helped the boys, who already began to undress. Then he helped me down. I guessed Aksel would usually strip too, but he kept his shorts on today for my sake.

We entered the water right below a miniature waterfall. The clear run-off from the mountain felt chilly. The beautiful ambiance still glowed from the morning sun. I imagined us as ancient explorers discovering this untouched pool.

The day had been Heaven to me and I didn't want it to end.

Later my grandma and I left Ingrid's to check on my mother. Mom felt well enough to take a shower. Grandma and I sat in her room and chatted about the cute Norwegian guys we had seen.

"Grandma! You're not supposed to look at guys! You're married," I said laughing.

Then suddenly a loud alarm sounded in the hotel. I opened the door and saw, towards the top of the wall, a red light blinking. Nobody told people to exit and there was no one around. Grandma ran to the lobby while I ran to the shower.

"Mom, I think the fire alarm is going off!"

"I don't care. I'm staying in this shower," she said firmly.

Eventually they turned off the alarm and the next day, though still sick, my mother got on the plane. Months later she found out she had Lyme's disease.

Now, seventeen years later in 2012, my mother's sickness was much worse. Her breast cancer from nine years ago had come back and spread. Then I remembered my Norwegian relatives. Jacob had died of leukemia at age five, yet Ingrid had given birth to a daughter after years of miscarriages. I had to believe that when God closed a door He opened another. Where was my open door?

Candle

Many wedding ceremonies include unity candles. Instead, I wanted a candle to represent my father.

<u>November 2001</u>

When I was 20 and attending art college in Minneapolis, I usually came home on the weekends; an hour drive. One weekend my parents had something to tell me. They told me to eat my dinner before we talked. I couldn't eat. I knew my dad was sick and the fact they were insisting I eat first couldn't mean good news. My stomach rebelled at every thought of food touching it, but I forced myself to eat.

"I'm done. Just tell me," I demanded of my mother.

"Let's go sit in the living room," she said.

I sat on the white couch that Mom never let me sit on when I was younger. Maybe that's why it still looked brand new.

"Dad has pancreas cancer," Mom said.

Dad explained further. "It's in stage four and has spread to the liver."

"Can't you remove the pancreas and get a liver transplant?" I asked.

"No. There is some chemo I can take but it's not effective in this final stage."

"How long do the doctors say you have?" I asked, expecting a measurement of years.

"Four to six months."

"What?" I asked, as tears came without permission. Hearing the word 'months' made me feel like sinking into the couch all the way to the center of the earth.

"No one can tell you when you will die," I said, climbing back up from the center of the earth, "only God knows that."

I hated seeing the pain that came with this disease, and with the treatment. First came blood clots in his legs that prevented him from walking, and with the blood clots came the risk of sudden death. Then came the nausea and then the back pain, tremendous back pain. I didn't want him to die, but I'd rather him die instead of being in this much agony. Sometimes I was afraid he'd die and sometimes I was afraid he wouldn't.

I sat in a chair by Dad's bed.

"I'm sorry I won't be around for the events in your life like your wedding day," he said sincerely.

"It's okay, Dad, it's only one day," I said. All I could think about was that he wouldn't be around for the rest of my life, so one day didn't seem to matter.

May 2002

Spring semester of my junior year of college ended in early May, so I stayed with my parents and spent time with my father.

Six months from diagnosis had passed, the chemo no longer did anything but make Dad sick; blood clots still lived in his legs, his stomach started to fill with fluid, and he used oxygen occasionally.

My father had two sons from his first marriage. My half brother, Mark, was ten years older than me. James was two years younger than Mark. I had never lived with Mark or James and only saw them a few times a year. Mark hadn't seen Dad since Christmas, over five months ago. Mark lived only two hours away, yet James, who had a nine-hour drive, came to see Dad often.

Dad had called Mark a few weeks before and said, "If you want to see me, now would be a good time. I'm not going to die tomorrow, but I'm feeling up to company now." Mark didn't come.

My dad's father had been to see my dad recently and saw how weak he was. My grandfather, a distant and light-hearted man who rarely used the telephone or told anyone what to do, called Mark and said, "Get down here and see your father."

Mark finally obeyed.

I wanted to take advantage of sketching my father from life before it was too late. I sat down on my parents' bed to draw him. He slept in the rented hospital bed by the window while I sketched. Dad never lost his hair to chemo, but it was now thinning and white, like his body. Mark arrived, so I quickly showed Dad my drawing which looked done, yet felt unfinished.

"It's good," he said.

I made my way out of the room so Mark could visit with Dad alone.

A half hour or so later, Mark came out of the room and into the kitchen with wet eyes. Having not seen Dad for five months, the progression of the disease shocked him. Maybe this fear was what Mark had been avoiding consciously or subconsciously these past months.

"Can you get me some smokes?" he said and handed me a ten-dollar bill.

His stocky body bulged out of his worn blue t-shirt and jeans. His hair, wet from sweat, stuck to his red forehead. Beer, Mountain Dew, Playboy, and cigarettes had masked his hurt for years.

That was the first time I saw my brother cry. The only memories I knew he had with Dad were a handful of fishing trips and nights jammin' on guitars. Surely he had more memories and probably regrets. Who was this brother of mine that felt like a distant relative but shared my wound—the wound of losing a father?

With his ten-dollar bill in my pocket, I left the house forgetting my purse.

"I'm sorry, I can't sell you cigarettes without an ID."

"I do not look seventeen! I'm twenty-one!"

"I'm sorry, but we card everyone who looks under 30."

"My fricken brother is thirty-one," I mumbled to myself as I left the store. I almost asked a lady if she would buy some for me. I knew Mark needed a cigarette right now more than anything. I hated letting him down.

I looked in the car mirror. Spots of acne and blotches of cover-up shined a shade brighter in the sun than my dyed, dirty blonde hair. I didn't notice the sun. There's no sun on days a parent is dying.

Mark stayed with a friend that night and came back the next afternoon to see Dad.

I didn't make it back in the room to finish my portrait. My mom and I left Mark alone to talk with Dad. Then we noticed the strangest thing. The door opened and my father came out and walked, slowly but confidently, into the kitchen and looked out the window.

Dad hadn't had that much energy for days. They say you emit great strength before death. Now I knew it was true. After my brother left Dad went back to bed and never got up. He had waited to see my brother before he could die.

I spent the later evening taking a bath and looking in the mirror, wondering who I was. My long and messy hair hung around my neck like a wet mane. My green eyes looked lost. Sometimes if I pulled my hair back, turned my head right, pursed my lips and squinted, I could see my father's face looking back at me.

I never heard my mother's voice on the intercom, only the growling of my stomach. I walked upstairs and opened the fridge, grabbing a piece of bologna.

"Kel?"

I closed the fridge.

"What?"

"Kel, come here, I didn't know where you were, I thought you went outside."

I walked into the room and my mom said, "I think it's time, he's dying."

I walked back into the kitchen and threw the piece of bologna in the trash. Right then I prayed every piece of bologna I saw after that wouldn't take me back to that moment.

My mom and I held my father's hands and watched his breathing fade. His spirit had already left--it was his fifty-three-year-old body that still fought for life. His body realized it was going to lose, and his chest rose with its last efforts to breathe.

The nurse from the hospice care arrived and pronounced him a few minutes later. A great calm came over my mother and me.

"Some have a much harder time leaving, they fight it," the nurse said. "You could tell he was ready to go."

"Why won't his eyelids close?" I asked her. I didn't like looking at my dad's body, his eyes half open.

"That's why they used to put coins on people's eyes back in the day," she said.

I tried to put a penny on his eyelid but it wasn't heavy enough.

"Mom, are you going to call the morgue?" I asked.

"Oh, it's late, maybe they aren't open. I can call tomorrow."

I knew I wasn't going to let her sleep alone tonight. "I'm not going to sleep in this room with a dead body in it," I said sternly and looked at her in the eye.

"Okay, okay, I'll call them," she said.

I didn't feel my father was there anymore; all I saw was a body. I didn't want it there reminding me of death, though I knew Mom wasn't ready to let him go.

I read in Joan Didion's <u>The Year of Magical Thinking</u> that when you die your pupils dilate. Your brain is no longer controlling your eye functions. That afternoon, my mother had mentioned going in to check on my dad and heard him talking in his sleep. She thought he was having a conversation with his dead brother. She heard him say, "Turn off the light, turn off the light." My mom thought he saw the bright light of Heaven but wasn't ready to go yet.

I wondered if people say they see light before they die because their brain is dying and their pupils dilate and let in light. I decided if our eyes are windows to our soul, dilating is our body's way of opening the windows and letting our soul out.

The entire month after my father died, I had to listen to my mother tell the details of his final two hours to people on the phone, people who came over, and even the mail lady. The sound of his heavy, broken breathing haunted me. I relived the moment over and over again until I became numb to it and it left my brain. Reliving it was miserable, but worth it not to be haunted anymore.

My uncle, my dad's brother, died seven years before my father. He died suddenly from a blood clot, without a hug for his daughter, without an "I love you, goodbye." Luckily I was able to say goodbye to my dad.

My friend's dad chose to leave her as a child. 20 years later he was dying and asked to see her. She said no. I was blessed to have a great father, if only for 21 years.

My dad was a healthy man. He played tennis once a week, exercised, and liked eating healthy foods. He never smoked and only caught a cold once every other year, if that.

As a boy he was teased and made fun of for his big glasses. He had bad eyesight since he was a baby, though it was that bad eyesight which saved him from going to war. He was called the math geek, the guitar nut, and the shy romantic who grew up poor and worked for everything he got. Frugal, he saved every penny. Dad worked for and invested in a medical company that, by chance, happened to be successful. He worked hard and shared his riches with many people.

When I was a baby my mother borrowed baby clothes, used cloth diapers, and made cakes for extra money, but by the time I was twelve I had been many places in the U.S. and Europe. I owed it all to my father, and of course my mother for convincing him to spend money on traveling.

Before Dad's funeral I leaned over the casket to put a guitar pin on his jacket. When I reached down to pin it, my father's arm raised up.

"Ahhh!" I screamed and turned away into my mother's arms as she stood behind me. I breathed heavy as my mother giggled and the startled funeral director apologized. I hadn't seen the funeral director on my right, grabbing my father's left hand to reposition his arm.

The funeral was the most uplifting funeral celebrating someone's life I had ever been to, and I had been to many. The song, "On Eagle's Wings," fit the tone and my dad's best friend gave a poignant speech. Instead of a melancholy atmosphere like most funerals, there was positivity and hope; a true celebration of life. Mom printed copies of the sketch I had done the day Dad died and gave them to everyone.

"unfinished" may 2002 Kelly Elly

Frankenberg, Kelly. <u>Unfinished</u>. 2002.

The worst part about the funeral, though, was the gravesite. I didn't know my mother and father had picked out a nameplate together. My mother's death year was missing but her name lay on the ground next to Dad's. Seeing my mother's name on a grave felt like being stabbed in the heart.

Cake

Donna and I wanted a bachelorette party. Our maids of honor agreed to throw us one last minute. "I didn't know what to do for a bachelorette party for two lesbians," Donna's maid of honor, Lori, said. "But then I realized you just do what you'd do for a guy."

Two weeks before the wedding, Lori and Alice threw us a Hawaiian-themed shower/bachelorette party. Pink and purple leis and fake palm trees decorated the private room at the restaurant. They made us wear coconut bras over our dresses and grass skirts and sunglasses with parrots on them. They even made us a boob cake.

There were two mounds of cake covered in light pink frosting that lay on a flatter surface to represent the stomach. Two dark pink chocolate rings topped off the mounds representing the nipples. A hole was made for a belly button.

After the dinner we went to a local dueling piano bar and sat on stage while two pianists played songs and made jokes. Word got around about the Bachelorette party. When Donna and I walked out of the piano bar area, a drunk lady in her late 40s came up to us and said, "Oh, Congratulations! Which one of you is getting married?"

"We both are," we said.

"When?" she asked.

"On May 6th," we said.

"On the same day?" she asked surprised and excited.

"We are getting married to *each other*," I said.

"We're kinda gay," Donna added.

There was a pause for the lady's drunk mind to process the information.

"Oh! Well, I am so happy for you two! Congratulations," she said, and gave us a double hug but didn't let go of our arms. "You ladies are so beautiful and I am so happy for you. I am a Republican but I have a gay nephew and I'm very proud. I believe you should be able to get married."

"Thank you."

"Ah, I'm just so happy for you," she said and hugged us again.

"Okay, we have to go, thank you," Lori said and pulled us away from the inebriated lady's grip.

"Okay, congratulations again and have a wonderful wedding!" she yelled loudly as we headed down the hall.

"On the same day," Alice laughed and shook her head.

It was a nice and respectable bachelorette party--unlike the one I had thrown my mother seven years earlier...

<u>Spring 2005</u>

Before Mom and Tom married, I thought it would be fun to host a bachelorette party for Mom. I would only invite her three sisters and we could watch a romantic comedy and it would be a nice girly party.

I purposely didn't invite my grandmother. Not that many people's mothers attend their bachelorette party. Mom agreed to attend the party but made it clear that she didn't want anything sexual. I knew my mother was respectable, yet open and honest. She could talk about sex, but she only got wild and joked about it when she drank a little wine-which was rare. This would not be one of those nights. Problems didn't start until Aunt Quiet showed up with my grandma.

"I invited myself!" my grandma said, giddy. I looked at my aunt and rolled my eyes. I loved my grandma; she was fun. Maybe it wouldn't hurt. I made some pasta and veggies and put cut-out magazine pictures of cute young guys in jeans and underwear in the middle of the table-nothing too dirty.

It turned out that Aunt Quiet, who I now call "Aunt Wild," and my grandma had stopped at the sex shop before coming to the party. They had picked up a bunch of dirty gifts for my mom and a pink cake in the shape of a penis.

"Oh no," I said under my breath to Aunt Giggly.

She gave me a look of full teeth to say, "Yikes."

Mom's face looked respectful though it said disgust. She opened each of the themed gifts. Edible candy underwear, a penis bouquet, orgasm sounds key chain, handcuffs, suckers, etc.

"The sign by the counter said, 'Ya, we know it's not for you,' and I told the guy, actually it's for me!" my grandma said, proud.

My eyes widened and I looked at my aunts. Until now I wasn't aware my grandmother was so explicitly sexual, and I would've liked to have died without learning that.

Mom stood and held the white plastic penis bouquet with a veil attached for a photo. She made a fake smile. Then she smiled the same smile while holding the penis cake. Everyone ate a tiny piece.

After everyone but my mother left, I said, "I didn't mean for it to be like this, I'm sorry."

"That's how it goes," she said. "I didn't want to feel gross about this. I don't want my wedding to Tom to feel gross. It's not about sex."

"I didn't invite Grandma," I said.

"I know. It's okay. You can keep all this stuff," she said as she left.

"What am I going to do with it?"

"I don't care what you do with it. Throw it out if you don't want it," she said.

I threw out the rest of the penis cake and I put the rest of the naughty gifts in a paper bag in the pantry. It had been in there for several months before I bumped the bag and remembered what was inside. Startled by a sound, I said outloud, "What the?...Oh." My foot set off the orgasm key chain.

*

Donna and I wanted an Asian style cake for the wedding. We chose a bakery in St. Paul that her brother had used for his wedding. There were many different fruit options, but we both loved mango.

Frankenberg, Kelly. <u>Cake Design</u>. 2012.

My mom and I used to decorate Christmas cakes and cupcakes for friends and neighbors. We even gave a cake to the mailman and the man who sold frozen food from a truck door to door. We stopped decorating cakes together the Christmas after Dad died.

For extra money when I was little, Mom sold cakes that she decorated for people's events. Even though she could draw any design with frosting on a cake, she never admitted she could draw or was artistic in any way. She made piano cakes for piano recitals, wedding cakes with layers, and flowers made out of frosting. There were retirement party cakes, Fourth of July cakes, welcome home cakes, graduation party cupcakes, birthday cakes with a Barbie doll sticking out of the top and the dress made of frosting. There were cakes for funerals, cakes for 80th birthdays, new homes, new babies, and showers. Truck-themed, cartoon-themed, business logos, college mascots, high school colors, fish, flowers, hearts, stars, quilts, over the hill cakes, and even boob cakes.

The smell of frosting lingered with me most of my life, so I rarely ate cake anymore. Yet I did love the creativity and mixing the frosting colors like a painter. I could write well with frosting and design a better cake than most of the store-bought cakes. It was something fun Mom and I did together, but Mom and I wouldn't be making my wedding cake like I had repeatedly fantasized.

Music

It was getting too last minute to find a harp player for the ceremony, and my friend Steve who played was going to be out of town. My dad would have played guitar at my wedding. He played at both of my brothers' weddings. I wanted a violin or a string instrument. A CD would have to do.

Having put it off until two days before the wedding, I finally sat down and purchased online a few versions of Pachelbel's Canon in D played on a harp. If I shortened it, the timing of walking down the aisle would be just right. I didn't want to stand there too long while the song finished. Paying close attention to those types of details creates less awkward moments. Like my mother, and a true girl scout, I was good at being prepared for just about anything.

When I went to pick up my wedding dress, I took the autistic boy who I watched with me. He was 12 and didn't talk much except a few basic words, so I turned on my iPod for the 45-minute drive. My iPod contained a random mix, chosen by iTunes since they all wouldn't fit, of about 800 or more downloaded songs, songs I wrote, and sound bytes I recorded. I turned it on shuffle. I focused on the road ahead while the autistic boy, Brandon, moved his fingers back and forth in the air like he was playing a floating piano. Then I heard my father's voice.

Out of hundreds of songs and sounds, I had only three recordings of my father's voice and I didn't know if iTunes had transferred any of them to my iPod. I had been listening to the list of music for a couple months and never heard my father's words on it until this day.

The recording was one he made on a mixed tape when I went to Norway when I was 14. Since he didn't come on the trip he made me a tape with songs I liked and recorded his voice at the end with a message. The message spoke more to me now than over 15 years ago when he recorded it.

"Hey Kel, this is Dad. Surprise, surprise. Hope you're gonna have a nice trip. I just thought I would come on here to say that I hope you have a great trip, and I'm gonna record these couple songs for ya. Sorry I couldn't find them all and I will certainly miss you, but have a wonderful, nice trip. I will see you when you get back on Sunday and you can tell me all about it. And after that we

94

can have some more fun summer with tennis and cabin and all those things. So love you, Hon, from Dad. See you, bye. And by the way, too, this next song from Pink Floyd, the words are, 'we don't need *any* education.' Haha. Ah, so here it is."

It wasn't just a beautiful coincidence. I had to believe the message came from Heaven on the day I picked up my dress for the one event my father was supposed to attend. Perhaps by trip Dad meant my life journey. My life journey was a trip, a trip away from Heaven, to which I would go back and be with him and have eternal fun; the summer fun a child always looks forward to, safe and warm with her parents. He was wishing me well.

And that sound byte didn't play randomly from my iPod again until the exact day I found out I was pregnant.

Rings

Five days until the ceremony.

Mom told me over the phone that her radiation had gone well but I wanted to know the results. A phone call was too cold, so I drove the hour to see her.

The usual greeting of "Hello," sang in the doorway. Sometimes my mother got so busy it would take her a half hour or hour into the visit before she would hug me. Phone calls poured in, sometimes every five minutes. She answered every one of them. When the news ended and the annoying sounds of commercials protruded the air, she turned the TV off. Tom was there like always.

"You want one?" Mom asked. "I bought these for my sisters."

She pointed at the pink ribbon rings on the kitchen table, the pink ribbon of breast cancer, the pink noose that choked the soul. It didn't matter, pink or black, thorns or no thorns, I didn't want one.

"No, thanks," I said, taking a seat in the kitchen.

"The radiologist is optimistic. They said the treatment is 80 to 90% effective. We just have to wait until it starts shrinking," Mom said.

I nodded as she finally told me what I had come to hear. But there was more.

"The doctor actually didn't tell me this until after, but there was a tumor on my brain, too, not just my skull, but they radiated it and it's gone. I don't know why she didn't tell me. I'm not going to tell my mom. I don't want her to worry."

A brain tumor now? Not just a tumor in her skull? I pictured my mom's body full of cancer, disintegrating away until there was nothing left of her. If there was one brain tumor, another could pop up again any time.

"The place on my hip was so small it probably only needs one treatment," she said and then pulled down her peach-colored shirt to show me the upper part of her chest. "They, ah, had to put in another port," she paused, "again, just like last time." I could tell that bothered her the most. The port of chemo, the point where poison enters the body, the front-line of a war for survival, the bitter reminder you can always feel in your chest.

Tom finally said something. "We heard they may make the chemo into pill form next year, the one she has to take every week for the rest of her life."

"That would be good," I said, looking at the wood floor, still in a shocked state.

"There are also some spots in my lungs, but they are very small and the doctor thinks they are just an infection from the steroids and should go away once my immune system gets stronger."

Spots on her lungs too? It just wouldn't end. Now the only thing left to do was pray. Pray to the God from whom I felt so distant. Was I asking for too much?

*

Donna and I found rings we liked on clearance. Both of us weren't big spenders when it came to jewelry. A Post-it love note meant more to us. Yet we wanted rings for the ceremony and the tradition of committing to each other. The ring I bought was white gold with the words "I love you" cut in it, and hers was yellow gold with the word "Love." They both lay flat with a small band of diamonds and a smooth band that twisted with the other one. Donna's ring needed to be resized, but with less than a week before the wedding there was no time.

"What do I do as a ring bearer?" Todd asked me.

"Well all you need to do is carry the rings and when the lady asks for them you give them to her," I told him.

"That's all?"

"Yep."

"Aww, I wanted to do more. Can I have a ring, too?"

"You want one? Sure, we can get you a ring, too," I said.

Todd had been accepting of me joining the family and moving in together, though he preferred his dad's house where he had spent most of his childhood.

The night my dad died, my mom told me to find his wedding ring before the guy from the funeral home took his body away. Dad had taken it off and put it somewhere when his fingers became bloated. He forgot where and Mom couldn't find it.

I walked into Dad's closet and up to his dresser. I opened the top drawer and saw plastic bags with various trinkets in them. I pulled one out that had some screws, paperclips, and odd things in it. It just so happened to also contain his wedding ring. I had walked right in and found it without effort.

"How did you find it?" my mother asked, shocked and relieved.

"I don't know," I said.

Two days before the wedding, I came down with a terrible cold. I started to lose my voice. The same thing had happened to my mom the day of her wedding to her second husband. Her laryngitis was so bad that she could barely say "I do." After her marriage ended she saw that as a sign that she shouldn't have married him. I hoped I wouldn't lose my voice.

When I was in Salt Lake City with Momtom before they married, Mom was having doubts about getting married. I had woken up in the middle of the night and couldn't sleep. I heard someone upstairs walking in the kitchen.

"Mom? What're you doing up?" I said as I came up the steps.

"Couldn't sleep. Want some tea?"

"Sure," I said.

We heard Tom snore. Mom closed the bedroom door which was right off the kitchen.

"I'm not sure I should get married again," she said as we walked to the living room.

"Why?" I asked as I sipped tea.

"Four marriages is a lot."

"So? Hasn't Elizabeth Taylor been married like seven times? If you love him, then marry him."

Our tea steamed in glass mugs on coasters atop the coffee table. We sat on the couch. Mom handed me a blanket.

"This is where we found out Dad was sick. He didn't even get to enjoy the place," she said looking around.

"I know. He didn't even get to go to the Olympics with us," I said.

We had driven to Utah with Dad during the 2002 Olympics, but he had been too sick to go to the events. I had to miss college and had asked one of my professors if I could miss two classes without it lowering my grade. I told her my dad was sick and this would probably be my last trip with him. She said she'd think about it. I stopped caring about grades after that.

"When I die, I want you to take off my ring with Tom and put on my ring with Dad," Mom said. "Your dad was the love of my life."

The darkness hid our watery eyes. We sat on the couch in silence while the sun came up over the mountains.

On Momtom's wedding day, May 1st, 2005, the sky dropped flakes of snow. My mother didn't wear white. She wore sea green. Her worries were gone. She was beautiful. She sparkled.

My grandma, my mom's mom, had breast cancer and had some of her breast removed the previous year. Mom stood by her on her wedding day for a photo.

"If we stand next to each other, together we have one set of normal breasts," Mom said.

"It's been a while since I've had boobs," my only grandparent without cancer said.

My dad's mom was referring to her sagging set that rested just above the pants she hiked way up. She had worn pants since the 1930s, attended business college, and traveled the world mostly on her own. She was the strongest woman I knew besides my mother. *"Stand up straight and stick your breasts out,"* Grandma used to tell me. Why did I want to have breasts so badly if they were going to fill with cancer and be cut off or sag down to my waist anyway?

"I miss Dad," I said to his mother that day.

"Me, too. But you know how much it hurts when you miss someone, so don't let your mind go there. You know you miss them and you leave it at that."

May 6, 2012. Wedding Day.

On the morning of Donna's and my wedding day it rained. Our backyard wedding dream would have to change like previous plans. Today was exactly 47 years after the tornadoes traumatized my teenage mother on May 6th, 1965. My voice had returned and I called Mom.

99

"I'm tired but I'm okay. I take a lot of breaks. Tom has done a lot. The yard looks so pretty," Mom said.

"Too bad we will probably have to get married inside," I said.

When we arrived at Mom's she had her hat on.

"I'm going to put my wig on later," she said. "Did you tan or something? You look orange."

"Ah, thanks, Mom. I know. It looks awful," I said, looking in the mirror on the wall at my first spray tan.

My friend, Holly, came just in time to do Donna's and my hair and makeup before the ceremony. Growing up in the same neighborhood, we lived at the end of the cul-de-sac and Holly's family lived on the end of the street. We started Kindergarten together and she slept over at my house many times and knew my parents well. I sent her parents a "Save the Date" card with a photo of Donna and I for the reception in June. Holly told me one of her dad's friends had come over and saw the photo of Donna and I on their fridge. He was Muslim like Holly's family and most Muslims don't condone that lifestyle. He made a comment about it and Holly's dad said strongly, "You can see those two people are in love. They deserve to be together and I support them."

Holly's Pakistani beauty was reflected in her long, thick eyelashes that almost looked fake.

"No, I don't want fake eyelashes," I told Holly.

"But they will make you look so much better in photos," she insisted.

"Yes. Sorry, I'm not a lipstick lesbian I guess." Though usually quite feminine, I wasn't used to much make-up.

While Holly did Donna's makeup, Donna's friend, Lori, helped me decorate the porch. We hung the large white paper cranes I folded from the steps of the spiral staircase and in front of the windows that spread from the ceiling to the floor. It had stopped raining but it was chilly enough to make us want to stay in the porch, especially since the porch was now beautifully decorated. We still could take photos outside in the brilliant green of the damp grass, the well-groomed flower pots hanging from the gazebo, and, best of all, the willow tree my dad had planted. Today I didn't care about snakes, ticks, or grass stains.

I put my dress on and pinned the last of the purple orchids on Donna's mom and sister while everyone, including the photographer, videographer, and officiant, gathered in the porch. Lori noticed the tag was still on my dress and help me cut it off. Then the wedding party all walked up the spiral staircase in preparation for descending. I yelled down to cue the music.

My father didn't walk me down the aisle and neither did Donna's. We both walked down the white spiral staircase from the turret to the wood floor of the porch, after our wedding party, to the sound of Pachelbel's Canon in D and squeaks from the staircase fluctuating.

Frankenberg, Kelly. Wedding Party Sketch. 2012.

"Good afternoon," said the officiant. She stood shorter than Donna and me. She was Asian, too, probably Hmong. Her baggy brown shirt and black pants didn't look formal or flattering. "The celebration you are witnessing today is the outward sign of an inward union of hearts. On this happy day we are gathered to acknowledge the true union that already exists between these two people."

Outside the porch windows the pine trees blurred their forest green shades with the misty air. There was barely enough room for our wedding party, all dressed in black except the flower girl, to extend across the porch in a line. Momtom sat directly across the porch by the entrance to the house. Donna's mom, her sister, and one brother filled the other wall. Her father didn't come.

"Whenever a family gathers to celebrate an important milestone in the lives of loved ones, there are those who, for a variety of reasons, cannot be present. Today is no exception. There are those we would wish to be here who are not. Among those absent family members, Kelly particularly wishes to remember and appreciate her father."

It had been almost exactly ten years since my father had passed. I missed him, but I left it at that and focused on the love all around me.

"For Donna and Kelly, this ceremony means that they will love each other day by day, taking each one as it comes. That they will be honest and communicate with each other, so unspoken thoughts are not misunderstood. That they will stand beside each other, when one is standing alone."

The Hawaiian flower and orchid bouquets stood out bright and colorful against the bridesmaids' dresses. The videographer positioned herself in the corner by the entrance to the house and Donna's family. While snapping pictures, the photographer moved around the floor and up on the staircase.

"That they will believe in each other and try to understand each other as best they can. That they will treat one another with care. And that they will continue to share their lives with each other as partners, as friends, and to go on building their future together. This ceremony expresses the spiritual bond that they experience together."

I tried to listen to the words the officiant said as my mind attempted to calm my nerves.

"Kelly, do you take Donna, to love and to cherish, to honor and comfort, in sickness and in health, in sorrow or in joy, in hardship or ease, to have and to hold from this day forth?"

"I do."

Donna's short royal blue dress with sequins on the crossing straps and chest fit her beautifully. My comfortable flip-flops sparkled with jewels that matched the jewels of my white dress.

"Donna, do you take Kelly, to love and to cherish, to honor and comfort, in sickness and in health, in sorrow or in joy, in hardship or ease, to have and to hold from this day forth?"

"I do."

Donna's niece, Quynh, the flower girl, wore a glittery lilac-colored dress. The same color fabric Asian take-out box purse held pink and purple rose pedals

102

which she dropped as she walked down the steps. Todd held a light blue fabric-covered take-out box which housed the rings.

"May I have the rings?"

Todd walked up to the officiant and pulled out the fortune cookie-like ring holder from inside the take-out box. His second-hand black pants, which were slightly too big, rested on his black shoes. His blue shirt beneath his black suit coat matched the fancy take-out box, as my meticulous planning made sure themes and colors matched.

"Let these rings be forever a symbol of the unbroken circle of love. Love freely given has no beginning and no end. May these rings remind you always of the vows you have taken here today and may these rings be blessed by the love with which they are given."

Donna had forgotten to take off her engagement ring. She quickly turned to Lori to help pull it off.

"Kelly, will you place this ring on Donna's finger and say to her, "Donna, I give you this ring as a symbol of my love for you."

I repeated the officiant's words and looked at Donna who was still turned to Lori trying to get her other ring off. I then glanced out of the corner of my eye and saw my mother. We weren't in Hawaii, we weren't in a church, but she was here and that's what mattered.

Donna finally turned around so I could put the ring on her finger.

"Donna, will you place this ring on Kelly's finger and say to her, "Kelly, I give you this ring as a symbol of my love for you."

As Donna repeated the words, I looked in her eyes. It felt official. We were finally getting married. I then turned to Todd and motioned for him to come forward.

"Todd," I said. "I want you to know that I love your mother very much, and I also love you very much. I want for us to be a happy family together. I promise to love your mother forever and I promise to also love you forever, too."

"Todd," the officiant said, "Do you promise to love and support your mother and her partner?"

He nodded and said, "I do."

I placed the blue tungsten ring on his finger.

"Do you like it?"

He smiled and nodded more than twice.

"By the authority of God and life itself, and by the day given to us to live, by the love of friends who honor and support this loving relationship and by the hurts and pain through which your lives have passed alone, by the long struggle of people for the freedom to love, and by the delight and hope you have found in each other, I recognize you as united in holy union. You may now embrace."

Our lips pressed together firmly for a moment before we wrapped our arms around each other. Donna and I were now married in every way that was important.

"Let us congratulate Donna and Kelly."

Clapping filled the porch. Tears and smiles reflected pieces of light and matched the glitter shine from our shoes and dresses. Dad's candle stayed lit throughout the ceremony. And for that moment I forgot about all the holes in my heart.

After the ceremony the smell of Asian food filled the kitchen. Shrimp and fried noodles. Pork and rice. Eggs rolls and spring rolls. Fish sauce and soy sauce.

My mother approached me, holding a long and skinny box.

"Someone gave this to me at my wedding," she said.

I opened the box. It was a long serrated gold knife with a shiny white handle engraved with the word, "Bride."

"I'm sorry I don't have more to give you," Mom said with tears in her eyes.

"No, Mom." I tried not to cry and hugged her. "You've given me everything."

I then looked at Donna. Her mom handed her an envelope. I heard Donna's mom say in Vietnamese that it was from her father. Donna opened the envelope. Inside were ten 100-dollar bills. Even though Donna's father didn't want to come to the ceremony, his gift recognized our commitment to each other. My smile met Donna's.

When the photos were finished, dinner was over, and everyone had gone home except Donna, Todd, and me, I saw my mom resting in the small indoor porch off the kitchen. She sat in the light pink reclining chair holding her rosary.

"That was a really nice ceremony," Mom said, with watery eyes.

"I'm sorry it wasn't very religious," I said.

104

"No, it didn't need to be," she said.

She paused and looked out the window and then looked at me.

"We should be able to love whomever we want. It shouldn't be about sex," she said.

Donna and I exchanging our vows in front of family and friends felt like a real wedding, legal or not. People could see we were in love. More importantly, my mother could too.

"I made Tom sit on the other side of me though because when you guys walked down the steps you could see up everyone's dresses," Mom said.

"Mom!" I smiled as I bent down to hug her.

May 7, 2012

That night Donna and I stayed at the Embassy Suites. The next morning we had breakfast in the dining area and the TV was set to CNN. The headline was same-sex marriage and how Mitt Romney didn't support it. Ironically, it hurt to finally be married and have the headline of opposition shoved in our faces.

Donna and I sat close on the same side of the booth as usual. There was an old lady looking at us with her judging eyes. "What are you staring at? Your grandkids gonna be gay," Donna said, though maybe not loud enough for the lady to hear. We laughed and ate our breakfast. Even if being gay in a Christian city in the middle of the Midwest wasn't always tolerated, it felt good knowing we chose to be who we are and chose to love.

The very next day President Obama voiced his support for same-sex marriage and my mother called me.

"Did you see the President supports your marriage?" she asked.

"Yes, Mom. That makes me happy." But I was happier for her excitement.

"I love you," she said.

"I love you, too, Mom."

With each day life will take away and life will give. I thought about my wedding day. My mother's presence on that day was the ultimate gift life could give.

I thought about my mother's smile and her generous heart. That was her essence.

Then I thought about the rainbow and the hope and happiness it represented with its ribbons of color. I realized the rainbow was still present that day, despite the lack of color in the bridesmaids' dresses. The rainbow was inside me.

PART TWO:
LEGAL MATTERS

One year later.

<u>May 14, 2013</u>

It was now official. Governor Mark Dayton signed the bill and this will allow us to get legally married starting August 1st. When we're legal we can get a mortgage on a house together without paying mortgage insurance. And when we have the baby currently inside me, we can both put our names on the birth certificate. These two simple things non-gay people might take for granted. Even though Donna and I had already committed to each other and had a ceremony, the benefits of being legal mattered to us.

This meant I would have to start planning a wedding, again.

I wrote my list. The same list as before:

Ceremony
Food
Photos
Dress
Hair
Shoes
Candle
Video
Invitations
Cake
Flowers
Rings
Music

<u>April 8, 2013</u>

I stood in my mother's living room again, but this time with Donna.

I had waited for Donna to come home from work to drive to Mom's together. I got the phone call before I got ready for work, the one that left me crying in bed alone.

"The chemo isn't working anymore, honey," Mom said over the phone. "The cancer is spreading."

"I thought they said they could manage it. How bad?"

"The doctor said I maybe have three months."

"No."

"I'm sorry."

"I'll come over. I'm sorry," I said, voice shaking by now.

"I love you. Drive safe."

"Maybe I'll have Donna drive with me. I'll let you know."

I called Donna while I walked around the kitchen trying not to cry. I had to wait for her to call off the rest of her workday and get home. I e-mailed my boss.

I was teaching college classes in Writing and Critical Thinking now and had to ask for another day off class last minute, as I had bronchitis the previous week.

My orphan nightmare was beginning, and this time I wouldn't be able to wake up from it.

Later that day, Donna and I stood in Mom's living room listening to her repeat what the doctor had said. Mom most likely wouldn't see the baby or our legal marriage.

But I couldn't give up hope so quickly.

110

Ceremony

"Woman is the artist of the imagination and the child in the womb is the canvas whereon she painteth her pictures." –Paracelsus

Before we got pregnant we called our future baby girl, Michaela, after my dad, Michael. We planned to choose the gender and use IVF from a clinic. I had always wanted a girl, and with my mother saving all my dolls, which filled up two rooms in her house, there was no question. After I finished my Master's Degree we were ready to start the process.

Wanting the baby to be both of our genes, Donna and I planned to use one of her brothers as the donor. But we had to decide which brother to ask. One lived in Vietnam, one was in jail, one was displaced, and one recently got married. Vinny, the one who got married was the youngest and cutest, but he was also not fond of going out of his way for others and had a new wife to consider.

The displaced brother, Jake, was Donna's favorite brother. He was honest and kind, but life circumstances didn't help Jake to fix his situation. He ended up living on the streets until one winter, cold and nowhere else to go, he agreed to let Donna bring him to our house. He didn't want to impose on us and said he would rather live on the street than inconvenience us, but we had room and wanted to help him.

He lived with us for a year before we were ready to ask him the big question.

"Jake, we have something to ask you," I said to him in our kitchen one night.

"Anything," he said.

"We don't want you to feel obligated and we want you to take a while and think about it, okay?"

He smiled awkwardly and asked, "What is it?"

Donna laughed.

Jake was about my height: a couple inches under six feet. His shiny, black hair hung a little above his ears that stuck out farther than normal. His long face mirrored his thin frame. Over forty, the lines on his face and sunken eyes showed years of hardship. His nostrils flared out beside the flat, Asian bridge of his nose. Rolling his cigarettes at the table, Jake's hands were gentle and careful.

"We were wondering if you would be able to help us have a baby by donating some of your sperm."

"Of course. I'd do anything for you guys."

"We want you to think about it, talk to your wife in Vietnam."

"I don't need to think about it."

I looked at Donna. She said some things in Vietnamese to him to make sure he understood my English correctly.

"You would just have a couple visits to the clinic for them to do some tests and collect a sample," I said.

"Sure, no problem."

Donna and I giggled from the awkwardness.

The clinic process, as we found out, was more complex when you have a known donor and want to pick the gender of the child. We were prepared for the high costs, but not the two three-hour psychologist appointments an hour away, over three days that we had to coordinate with Donna's, mine, and Jake's work schedules. Then there was the lawyer we had to go with through the company. They charged $1,000 just for signing the donor paperwork and we still had to drive an hour away.

The appointments started becoming too much for our schedules and pocketbooks, and then there was talk of quarantining the sperm for several months before we could start. Donna and I talked.

September 2012

"I don't necessarily have any fertility issues, and Jake already has two children in Vietnam," I said.

"I don't care anymore if it's a boy or girl," Donna said.

"I guess we can try on our own. And if it's a boy we can save that IVF money for adopting a girl in the future. I just want to have a baby."

"Ok, then let's do it on our own."

The entire process became very convenient with Jake living in our basement. Since he was a smoker, I asked him a few days prior to ovulating not to smoke much. Then on the nights we would try he would let us know when the cup of life was on the table by saying, "Ok, I'm going out for a smoke now!"

112

On the nights we had Todd, Donna would entertain him while I tried my best with a 4-inch syringe from Target. Other times Donna would assist. I would elevate my lower half afterwards to allow gravity to help in the process.

This went on for seven months, once a month.

"I think we should try two days in a row this time," I said, after the sixth month. "And I'll elevate longer."

We hated bugging Jake, and this month I had to teach an art class the night I was ovulating. We were getting anxious and Mom's health seemed to be declining. Donna and I worried Mom would die before I got pregnant or before she could meet her grandbaby.

Then Jake told us some bad news. He owed a fine to the county that he still couldn't afford to pay back with his temp job. He would have to stay in a work house for several weeks to do his time. They let him out to go to his job, but it was an hour commute so he only had time to go to and from work. We wouldn't have time for the "baby project" for a month or two.

Donna and I were disappointed, but there wasn't anything we could do.

A few weeks later I took a pregnancy test and both the negative symbol and the positive symbol appeared, but much too quickly this time. I figured it was defective and decided to wait.

A few days later I took another test and it was negative. I tested again later, it was also negative. Wanting to be pregnant so badly, I researched test results online. I found out a test can appear negative if you drink a lot of water, which I had that day, and also it's likely to have false negatives, but less likely to have a false positive. I waited until morning to test again.

Morning came and Donna went to work. I slept in and then tested. Positive. I took a photo and sent it to Donna.

"Really?" Donna said hopeful when she was able to call me.

"I'm going to go into the doctor today to confirm. Hard to know with two negatives and one positive," I said excited.

"Wish I could go with you," she said.

"I know. It's okay."

My best friend Alice had been trying for two years with her husband. She said it wasn't fair how some people just do it once and they can get pregnant, when others struggle for years. I was hoping we weren't one of those who would

113

struggle. Seven months seemed a long enough wait for us. Being pregnant now would be perfect timing with Jake gone and Mom's health.

Since Donna couldn't use her phone much at work, I texted her from the clinic to call me. In the meantime I called Mom

"I'm pregnant, Mom! I'm due on Halloween!"

"I'm so happy and excited for you honey! Finally!"

It was February, 2013.

*

May 2013

Donna and I were lucky to get on a list early enough to have our ceremony officiated by the Mayor of Minneapolis, Mayor R. T. Rybak, instead of a judge. City Hall would be our venue, August 1st, while other gay couples had the option of getting married at the Como Zoo Conservatory in St. Paul.

The Mayor would have to speed through each ceremony to make sure to get everyone, but of course not so quick that it wouldn't be heartfelt.

Donna and I wanted to write our own vows again.

Donna confessed to me one night.

"I was researching lesbian vows online, but I had a typo and 'lesbian cows' came up."

"I dare you to say that to the mayor!"

"Don't dare me. I'll do it."

While writing my vows I remembered writing my mother's eulogy. I wrote her eulogy while Aunt Giggly helped my mother write her own obituary.

"I'm 61, not 62," Mom corrected Aunt Giggly when she was reading it back to her.

"I know," Aunt Giggly said with a sarcastic yet sweet chuckle, "but I was hoping you would make it to your next birthday."

There was a pause and then they laughed together as they always had, yet it also seemed a way to release the hurt this time.

I saw the hurt in my aunt's expression. I felt it. My mother raised her. She was losing a mother, too, like me.

These days of preparation for my mother's funeral while she was still alive became strictly about expecting a death instead of a wedding or a baby.

Speaking at a wedding is similar to speaking at a funeral. The audience is family who are either very happy or very sad, the random friends you met throughout life, and the few people you kind of recognize. The only difference in the audience, besides the tone, is that wedding guests are invited and funeral guests are not. Of course family is obligated to attend both, but those who come to your funeral perhaps are your true friends.

Food

Funeral food only tastes good if you're pregnant or starving, because your brain is not in a state to enjoy food. Eating becomes a motor function. The same goes for a wedding if you are the bride. You spend most of your time focused on your guests, kissing when the glasses clink, smiling for photos, drinking cheap or expensive champagne...or if you're pregnant, *not* drinking champagne... Eventually the choice of food becomes about the guests and what they would like to eat.

Since our legal wedding was in the middle of the night, the hotel down the street from City Hall claimed to have an appetizer buffet until midnight and drinks until 2 a.m. The thought of another reception and party after another ceremony was tiring, especially in the middle of the night, and especially for a pregnant woman of seven months. Wedding cake would be our food...that's if anyone wanted any at 3 a.m.

When my father was dying my mother and I went through the stages of grief in a week. We surprisingly came to acceptance quickly. I think it was because of our personalities and not having much choice in the matter except how we dealt with it.

But this time I was losing my last parent and couldn't go to acceptance. Nobody else I knew was going through that so I felt alone with my grief. There was no use for denial so I went through a stage of bargaining.

April 2013

My friend had told me about this guy in Canada who made medicine out of pure cannabis, or marijuana, that cured his cancer. It was concentrated into oil that you ingested on your tongue. If I found that and gave her some would it help? If only we could get Mom some drugs she might get better or have less pain.

Trouble was marijuana was illegal. The guy's website talked about how you could purchase the seeds and grow the plant and make the oil yourself, though if you didn't do it safely it could easily start a fire. There was no time for that and no time to be risky and mess with that, legal or not. What could I do?

Then I thought for a moment. When I studied writing in Scotland I remembered a few of the students smoking pot, and one of them talking about having it in California where she lived. Grass Valley, California was my new goal.

So I called her to find the strong, pure kind my mother could ingest.

"My friend makes some in banana bread and the oil," she said. "But you would have to come here to get it."

Obviously I couldn't fly it home on an airplane; even with banana bread it would be too risky. I wasn't the kind of person to break the law besides speeding, but I was desperate. Explaining to my mother why I wanted to take four days and drive to California and back while I was pregnant wouldn't go well. I didn't know who else to ask to do it.

Also if Mom only had a few good days left, why would I want to spend them away from her? What if something happened to her while I was away? What if I got arrested and put in jail?

Even though I was an adult, I felt I had to follow my dying mother's demands. But even if I went, how was I going to convince her to take it?

Getting Tom on board first would help.

I mentioned a little bit to him, but I didn't get a chance to finish. I also didn't get a chance to tell him not to say anything to her yet.

Donna and I had been staying with Mom for a weekend to spend some time with her. I walked in Mom's bedroom later to check on her.

"I'm not letting you go to California. You'd be wasting your time. I'm not going to take any drug."

"What?" I looked at Tom, pissed. "Why did you tell her? I wasn't done explaining it yet," I said to Tom.

I then turned to Mom. "You haven't heard it yet. Can you just hear me out please?"

"No," she said, "I'm not going to smoke anything. I have cancer in my lungs."

"You don't have to smoke it, Mom, you just ingest it on your tongue or eat banana bread."

"You don't even know if it works."

"It works differently in everyone, but it doesn't have side effects and it can help with nausea when your medication can't. No one has ever died from it."

"No, I'm not going to take it."

"Just because it's illegal in Minnesota? It's not illegal in California."

"I don't need it, honey. I'm dying. I'm okay with that. You need to be okay with that, too."

"I am okay with it, but if it can help some of your symptoms, why not try it? It can't hurt. Please?"

"It's not a good idea for you to go."

"What if someone else can drive it here? Then would you just try a little?"

"What if it makes me sick? You don't know what's in it."

"I trust my friend," I said.

Mom had smoked pot once in her day just as my father had also tried it. Both said it made their heart race and they didn't like it. Going to an art college I was one of the few who never tried it. I was only ever offered two or three times and said no. I liked being in control of my body and didn't like to do anything illegal. The main reason I never tried pot, though, was because I knew my children would ask me some day and I wanted to be honest with them. I wanted to show them that you can say no, it's that easy. If I can say no, so can others.

"You are upsetting me now," she said. "I don't want to feel like this, especially if I don't have that much time left."

I left the room crying. Donna had tried to pull me out of the room sooner, but I needed to finish the conversation.

"See, now you are all upset. If you need to we can talk about this tomorrow, but I'm not sure I will change my mind," Mom called.

I recognized the stress in her voice the way she would yell when I was a teenager. But this time it was weaker. I couldn't heal her, but I could try this. This was the one thing I could do for her. Why wouldn't she just let me do it? I would regret it for the rest of my life if I didn't at least try.

I called as many friends and family I knew who lived in California and Utah. My brother James lived in Nebraska, but he was a cop. I would ask him only as a last resort.

When I finally found a cousin willing to drive it half way, I couldn't get a hold of my friend in California.

"I don't want to take it, honey," Mom told me the next time we talked about it. "Plus you can't even get it here."

"What if I can? Will you at least try a tiny bit if you have pain or nausea?"

"Maybe. That's the best I can do, okay? Why don't you get advice from our nurse friend, Jane, and Ron, he's a pharmacist," she finally said, maybe just to shut me up.

"Ok," I said.

Donna and I went home that week so we could go back to work and have Todd stay with us. It was exhausting going back and forth the hour drive, worrying, driving, and trying to have a life while spending time with Mom.

Meanwhile, I kept on with my mission and called Ron.

Ron was on board with it. I called Mom to tell her the news. I was excited.

"Okay," was all she said.

I came back to Mom's house for the morning before I taught classes. Her friend Jane happened to be visiting and I ran into her on my way out of the house. I briefly explained my plan to her.

"In my years working as a nurse I've never seen it do much. Otherwise they would have it available. I'm probably not the best person to ask because I'm not an advocate for it," Jane said, not as pragmatic as I hoped she would be.

Hope sank with my face. Jane could tell I was disappointed but she was firm in her belief. I didn't want her to tell my mother her point of view, but I had left before I could tell her not to.

I would still try. I had to. I had found a way to get it to Salt Lake City. I just needed to get it the rest of the way, or even to Iowa or Nebraska where I had more family.

A week went by and my friend in California called back to see if I was able to convince my mother to let me go get it.

"If we got it she won't take it," I said.

"I'm sorry," she said.

"I'll let you know if anything changes."

So disappointed, now the thought of banana bread, with or without pot, made me sick.

The two things in life I desperately wanted more than anything this year— to get married and to get my mother medicine, both weren't legal yet in Minnesota.

Even if I had been able to get the marijuana, it would have been too late. Mom went downhill fast.

These days I kept my phone on vibrate instead of silent overnight in case there was an emergency.

Then, there was.

Tom called the morning after my mother's surgery. The surgery was supposed to close off an artery that was causing her to cough up blood clots from her lungs. I had gone with Momtom to the hospital. Watching her get in and out of the building, the hospital bed, and the car was like watching an 80 or 90-year-old, and my mother was only 61.

I had seen my dad become an old man, too. If this is how it felt, I didn't want old parents. However, it was too late. They were old and dying right before my eyes. I now lived the orphan nightmare every night and every day.

After the surgery Mom seemed much weaker. I just prayed that the coughing would subside. She wasn't even a smoker. I cursed the smokers. How could anyone smoke if they could feel what it would do to them and their family in the future? My mother didn't deserve this. Nobody did. And their children didn't, either. I could only pray the baby inside me would never have to see me go through that…yet I would be lucky to make it to 40 with my genes.

"She's really out of it, ah, I can't seem to get her to respond. I don't know what to do. Can you come over?"

"Ok," I said to Tom. "We'll be right over. I'll call my aunt, too."

"I didn't want to bug her, but I don't know what to do. I can't get your mom out of bed."

"I'll call you when we are in the car," I said and hung up.

Luckily, Donna was there to distract my mind from picturing driving an hour to find my mother dead.

And that was not the case when we got there.

Aunt Giggly had beaten us there.

Mom was on the couch.

"I couldn't get her to wake up," Tom said. "She was fine this morning. She got up and then lay back down on the couch."

"She seems much better but I'll call the nurse," my aunt said.

I walked over to Mom.

She opened and closed her eyes slowly.

"Can you sit up, Mom?"

120

She tried to sit up. Donna helped her.

My aunt walked back in the living room, or dying room, rather.

"The nurse said it was probably the Oxycodone she took last night after the surgery. She should be fine now."

Mom looked more awake and with it.

"I don't know what happened," Mom said.

"I couldn't wake you up," Tom said, less panicked now.

Seeing Donna breathe out her sigh, I breathed out mine, too.

My tense shoulders finally let down and relaxed as much as they could.

I couldn't handle the stress of being an hour away when something happened.

"I think I should stay here for a few days at a time," I said.

"Okay," Donna said.

Photos

I read the description of what would be provided at our August 1st wedding. We were allowed one free photo. That wouldn't be enough for us to document this once (or twice) in a lifetime event. I went through the first ceremony's potential photographer emails and found one willing to work the early morning hours.

Summarizing a life with photos on a board is challenging. We pick the ones from childhood, graduation, wedding, family, hobbies, pets. The ones with the biggest smiles, the ones that capture the essence of the person. Since a funeral, in my mother's words, is essentially a celebration of the person's life for the people who are still living, you want to pick pleasant pictures that draw positive emotional responses.

Surprisingly, going through photos of my mother wasn't making any of us cry. Aunt Giggly and Aunt Quiet sat at the dining room table flipping through albums and making the montage for my mother's funeral. Uncle Quiet had come over to support Aunt Quiet. He stood around and took orders from all of us. Tom printed photos from his computer, Donna helped cut paper, and I found items to display at the funeral. At this point, Mom was still alive, but we didn't have much else to do while she napped. And Mom loved nothing more than to be prepared, even for her own funeral.

Just two days ago my friend Holly paid a photographer to come to the house to take pictures of Mom in her last days, having no idea that those last days would be just a few.

The photographer took photos of my mom with her family members who came to visit. The best ones were of her and me, her hand resting on my exposed pregnant belly of three months. The photos captured a melancholy tone. It was like the gloaming, where the sun shines a bittersweet brightness before it disappears with the pull of the sunset. Her eyes locked with mine in a black and white photo that would be the last photo our living bodies would share, and the only photo of her with her grandbaby she would never meet.

The night ended with a few more visitors. Mom's brother who had been out of touch came to see her later in the evening. She had been waiting to say goodbye to him as my dying father had waited for my brother.

The doctors had told us maybe three months. So far it had only been a month, but we saw the end nearing. Would she have pain? Would she linger on or leave us quickly?

"I want to die tomorrow, May 9th," she said, "on my father's birthday."

"Don't go yet, Mom," I said. "I want you to see the photos."

Later that day I got a text from a friend and ran into Mom's room.

"Mom! The House is voting on the freedom to marry. They are thinking it's going to pass!"

"Turn on the news!" she said with as much enthusiasm as she could muster.

But when I came in later she was sleeping.

I took advantage of her sleeping: one last life drawing.

Frankenberg, Kelly. Unfinished, Too. 2013.

<u>May 9, 2013</u>

Today a bipartisan majority of members in the Minnesota House of Representatives voted "yes" on the freedom to marry for same-sex couples.

It was the day of her father's birthday, the day Mom wanted to die. She was in a discomfort, which the hospice nurse called a sort of pain. Her weak body felt extremely uncomfortable in every position. She couldn't move much, so we took turns trying to move her around in the confining hospital bed which sat in the same spot in her bedroom where my father's had sat; right between the window and the regular bed.

The hospice nurse stood on the window side of the bed while the rest of us, Tom, Donna and I, and my two aunts, stood between the beds.

"Honestly, since you aren't eating," the nurse said to my mother and then to us, "and she isn't taking much water, it's only going to be a couple days or fewer. I can give you something to relax your muscles, but you won't be responsive. It will help ease the pain of your throat and your discomfort."

"Yes, I'm ready for it now," Mom said

Her blood had been clotting too much in her nose that chunks of it came down the back of her throat. She choked a little on them and needed help pulling them out. Tom, the nurse, and I took turns.

Since she would be unresponsive, we all said our goodbyes before she took the medicine.

Barely able to lift her arms, I bent down and hugged her.

"Do you have any regrets?" I asked her the same question I had asked my father before he died.

"I wish I would have yelled at you less," she said.

"It's okay, Mom. I love you."

"I love you too, honey," she said slowly.

"If Dad comes to get you, talk loudly so I can hear what you're saying to him, okay?"

She nodded.

After she took the meds she slept for a bit and didn't talk or move much. She was breathing and moaning a little in her sleep. Finally, at 6 p.m., the priest she liked arrived to give her last rites.

Donna and I sat on the bed with my two aunts and Tom sat in a chair next to Mom's bed.

"Hello, Brenda, I'm Father John and I'm here with you," he said quite loudly.

All our eyes widened like a mummy had come alive as Mom lifted her hand and turned her head to him, her first movement since the medication. She couldn't speak or open her eyes but she knew he was there.

"Let us pray," he said. "In the name of the Father, the Son, and the Holy Spirit."

Mom raised her arm to make the sign of the cross, but she couldn't lift it any higher so Tom moved it for her.

That night she moaned in her sleep. I hoped she wasn't in pain because we were already giving her pain med doses. I wanted her to pass away on her dad's birthday like she wanted. I had prayed so much she would live and now I was praying she would die, just like I had with my father. There was the point-the point of dying where it's time to cross over.

Everyone else was asleep. Donna was asleep in my old bedroom in the basement. Aunt Giggly was in the bedroom next to her. Aunt Quiet slept on a blow-up bed in the living room. Tom was asleep in the bed in their room, snoring.

I put a sleeping bag on the floor so I could stay with her. I wanted to be with her the moment she passed, but I couldn't stand the moaning sounds her chest made when she breathed and I was too exhausted mentally to sit there all night.

"Should we give her more meds?" I asked Tom, waking him up. "Sorry, I don't like the sound she's making. Um, I didn't wanna wake you."

"Ah, no, it's okay. Yes, let's give her some more."

I looked at the clock, 12:45 a.m.

"She didn't die on her dad's birthday."

"You go sleep. I'll let you know," he said.

The next morning she was still breathing but slower and no moaning. Aunt Giggly had to go drop off her car for her daughter to use and Donna went with her. Tom did some work outside and Aunt Quiet and I took turns in the kitchen and sitting with Mom.

I sat by my mother and I looked at her eyes. They looked dilated like my father's had looked after death. Tom talked to her like she was still alive, but I knew she was gone. Did her body just keep taking breaths since it had been breathing every second for 61 years and didn't know how to stop without slowing down first?

I whispered to her, "Mom, I love you. You can go now."

Then I remembered something from my childhood I had forgotten about since my father died. For some reason, when I was little, I decided that after a person dies if you say 100 Hail Mary prayers the person can go up the 100 steps to heaven.

I started saying them.

Once I finished the last one, I noticed my mother's breathing had slowed dramatically. Aunt Quiet came in and sat with my mom.

"I better get Tom," I said.

Just then the door to the garage opened and Donna and Aunt Giggly were back.

"It's time. She's breathing slower. Can you call for Tom?"

I went back in the room and Tom came in from outside, threw his jacket on the floor and ran into the room.

Tom and my aunts stood on one side of the bed and Donna and I were on the other.

"The hospice nurse will be here at noon to give you a bath," Aunt Giggly told Mom.

She then took one more breath.

"I think she's gone," I said.

"I guess she really didn't want that bath," Aunt Giggly said.

Sobs that we were holding in exhaled out, resembling some kind of laugh.

We looked at the clock. Noon, right on the dot.

"She missed Grandpa's birthday," I said.

"May 10th," Tom said to her, "That's your day."

I left the room right away like I had when my father passed. She was gone; there was nothing left but a body. Donna hugged me and we went outside for a walk. My aunts gave Tom some privacy. We heard him yell my mother's name loudly.

Then he sobbed.

126

I tried not to let it echo in my head as Donna and I walked, passing the hospice nurse driving in. The clouds opened to let in the spring sun after the endless Minnesota winter.

Dress

The idea of black dresses for our bridesmaids were more funereal to me now than ever.

"Can we not have our wedding party wear black this time?" I asked Donna. "I'm just worried no one has one in similar colors and no one wants to buy one."

"They don't have to match that closely," she said.

"Yes they do. If they are too similar but not matching they will clash and look retarded. I'm a painter, I know," I said.

"Maybe blue," Donna said.

"Maybe."

After a long pause I looked at Donna.

"Can we go buy an outfit for Mom's funeral? When my dad died my mom and I went shopping for clothes to wear to the funeral. I don't want to wear black," I said. "Maybe something bright and colorful. Hawaiian. Mom liked Hawaii."

Two months later.

I walked in the closet and pulled out my wedding dress that we still hadn't dry cleaned from the reception last year. I tried to squeeze it on over my pregnant belly of five months. I couldn't zip up the back, and by the legal ceremony my belly would be twice as large. It fit if I just didn't zip it.

Looking online at maternity wedding gowns and numerous stores, I felt worried that I wouldn't find a dress in time. My belly wasn't big enough to make me look pregnant, so the dress styles just made me look fat.

"You're not fat...you just *act* fat," Donna said to me one night.

"Thanks," I said with a huff.

I tried on my dress again. It just needed some lace-up strings in the back to hold it up and look like it was naturally supposed to tie like that. I sketched some ideas.

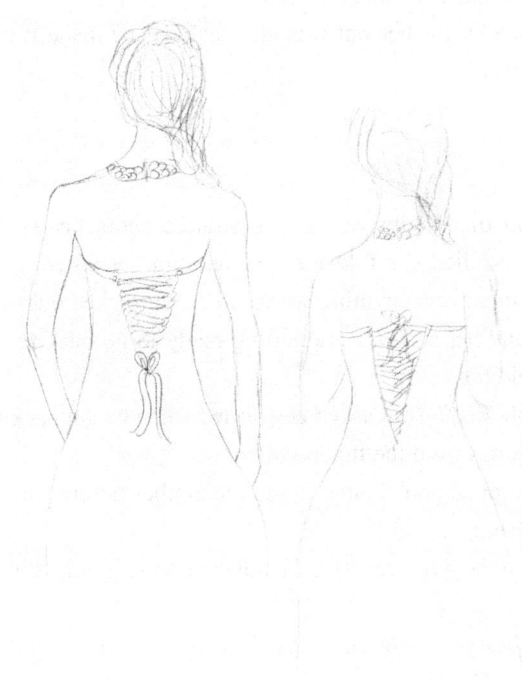

Frankenberg, Kelly. <u>Dress Designs 2</u>. 2013.

If I tried to do it myself it might be disastrous. Mom would've been the best person to ask.

My best friend, Alice, had a mother passionate for sewing also. I could ask her mother, Carrie.

Carrie was happy to help out. I came by after she had returned from a trip to Florida.

"How was Florida?" I asked her as she measured my back for the dress opening.

"It was okay. I feel bad for my sister, though; she will have the hardest time now that my mother is gone."

"Alice didn't tell me your mother died! I'm so sorry," I said, turning around and hugging her. "I know what it's like to lose a mother and it's hard at any age."

I felt sympathy for her but was also jealous she made it to her age before she lost her mother.

*

After mom died, Tom was acting strange about her clothes leaving the house. Before she died she told me, Donna, and her sisters to go through her closet to see if there was anything we wanted. We picked out some clothes, and after she died and her sisters were getting ready to go back to their houses, we pulled out the clothes.

"What's all this?" Tom asked concerned when he got back from picking up the last of the things from the funeral home.

"You mentioned you wanted to see the clothes before we take them so you know who got what," I said.

"Why do you have to do this now? You're going through her things already?"

"Ok, well do you want us to leave them here for a month and then come back and get them?" I asked.

Mom's sisters could tell the situation was getting awkward.

"That's okay. We'll leave them," they said.

"No, Mom said you could have them," I said.

"I don't know," Tom said, flustered.

I didn't understand why her sisters couldn't just take the clothes Mom had told them they could have. There was still a huge walk-in closet full of clothes even after we went through it.

Tom wasn't ready to let them go.

"It's not like he's going to wear them," I whispered to my aunt.

"He's just not ready," Aunt Giggly, now "Aunt Sad," said.

"I'm taking this dress," Aunt Quiet said, "she said I could have it. I'll send Tom a photo of it later if he wants to know."

That night I dreamed I was an Elizabethan queen and married the Frankenstein monster but he didn't know he was a monster.

Hair

Having to have a wedding all over again made me want to be cheap the second time around. My friend Holly deserved to be paid for her professional hair and makeup services, but her company was luxury level expensive that even her friend discount seemed too pricey for a second wedding. Negotiating price with friends is awkward.

"I think we'll just get our make-up done with you and we can get our hair done at the place down the street," I said to Holly over the phone.

"No, nonsense, why would you do that?"

"It's cheaper and more in our budget."

"Just tell me your budget and we'll make it work. I want you gals looking the best!"

"But your services are worth more than that," I said.

"No, it's okay. It's you!" she said. "What kind of style do you want?"

"Just curls with flowers like last time."

I offered to create some paper crafts for one of her company's events in exchange for the larger discount on her service.

*

A few days before Mom died, I stood in her walk-in closet, trying to find a dress she could wear to be buried in and for the open casket.

"How about this one?" I asked, holding it up so she could see from the bed.

"No," she said slowly, tired.

"This one?"

"No."

"This one?"

"Oh, I don't even think I wore that once. That one will probably be okay," she said.

I hung it on the door. I felt excitement for a moment. It was like we were getting ready to go on a trip together and I was helping her pack...although she only needed one outfit.

"I think I should wear a wig. What do you think?"

131

"I like you better without fake hair. I think it would look more natural if you just had a hat on. Maybe the black one and we can pin one of your flowers in it?"

"That sounds good," she said.

For certain things I preferred fake flowers over real flowers because it was one more thing you didn't have to watch slowly die.

Shoes

The thought of picking out shoes for my mother to wear for the funeral was strange because they were shoes she would never walk in and the last pair her feet would ever wear.

"How about these?" I lifted them up for her to see from the bed.

"If you think they still fit me."

She had already given most of her shoes to Donna. I didn't fit in her shoes; my feet were too big.

Before the wedding my feet were swollen. I didn't think I would be able to fit in my white jeweled flip-flops from the ceremony last year. The only shoes in the house I could wear were my blue crocs, and there was no way I was going to wear them to the wedding! I tried them on anyway.

"Now that's really gay," Donna said, laughing.

I then remembered how swollen my father's feet had become, and the pain I created just forcing his shoes on.

December 2001

A week before I turned 21, a month after they told me of my dad's diagnosis, my mother went out of town for a wedding. I agreed to stay with my father and take care of him for the weekend. I slept downstairs in my old bedroom.

Usually a light sleeper, I slept my hardest.

Then something forced me to awake, though I was so physically exhausted by the sleep, I couldn't move. Eventually a noise was discernible, though I couldn't tell what it was. Was I in a dream, a nightmare?

The buzzer kept beeping. It was somewhat loud. Why didn't I wake quicker? The buzzer again. My dad needed me. What could possibly be wrong that he needed me at 4:30 in the dark morning? I panicked. How long had he been buzzing? I took this long to wake, had I missed minutes of endless buzzing? Did he lose faith that buzzing would work? I saw myself outside of myself, like I was watching myself in a movie. I jumped out of bed like an actor responding to a cue.

I ran down the hallway in the dark. I entered my father's room before I realized I ran up the steps. He sat, crouched over awkwardly on the bed, one hand by the buzzer. He made a sound of pain.

"What's wrong? How long have you been buzzing?"

"About five minutes or so."

What? Tears tried to come out. What would keep this man buzzing for five minutes?

"What's wrong?"

"My back," he started to say, but then made another sound that was somewhere between a grunt and a cry.

"What can I do?"

"I think we need to go to the hospital."

I didn't understand. He was fine. My mother made sure. *She made sure he was fine.* He told her to go to the wedding that weekend, that he would be okay, that I could take care of him, it was only a weekend.

"Okay," I said, surprisingly calm. I could see myself telling my mother, *Look what happened when you left, look what I had to do.* I imagined that the crisis had already passed. I had already been there and taken care of it. But it was happening now.

"I'll need my license. It's on the dresser."

"What's a dresser?" I panicked. I couldn't process the word. I thought, oh no, I don't know what a dresser is, we're screwed. Yet the panic only lasted for one sentence.

"In the closet," he said, barely moving an inch on the bed.

I knew what he was talking about now. I even laughed a bit thinking it was funny to forget what a dresser was.

He needed his socks and shoes. His socks seemed ten sizes smaller than his feet. Every little push of the sock caused pain, then the shoes. I tried to hurry.

"I'm sorry," I said as I forced in his foot like a child's in a shoe two sizes too small.

"It's okay," he whispered, holding in the pain.

I closed my eyes for a second and hoped my deep breath would act as a pep talk.

I then grabbed the wheelchair he hadn't needed but once before.

It took all his energy just to sit in the chair. I tried not to imagine putting him in the car. I had never witnessed anyone suffering with this extreme pain. Yet he was himself, strangely so. His intelligence and sense of calm remained. It was like he was saying, "Everything's going to be okay, don't worry about me," with only his presence.

I offered to call an ambulance, but he didn't want that. Perhaps it was the extra money on the hospital bill. Because my father grew up poor, saving ten dollars was a victory, no matter how much money he made.

I looked at his face; no tears, thank God. Once I sat him in the car I thought everything was going to be okay. He knew how to get to the hospital, and there shouldn't be traffic this early. Yet every little turn hurt him.

I kept focused on the road but took a quick glance at him. His once tan face was now pale and sunken. Hair that was turning gray was now entirely white and thinning more. His blue eyes only reflected gray and his skinny body made him look like my great-grandfather.

I tried to drive slowly not to harm him with the bumps in the road, but I wanted to get there quickly. The conflicting desire to drive slow and fast at the same time ate away at me as I drove. I drove my mother's Lexus, one of the smoothest riding cars on the road, and yet it didn't help Dad's extreme discomfort. I wished I could call Mom, yet she'd be upset and there was nothing she could do from two states away.

We arrived at the hospital and found the emergency entrance. A small town hospital at five in the morning is basically deserted, so I had to push a buzzer to get in. No one came to the door.

Finally the door opened and I ran inside. It looked empty.

"Hello!" I screamed.

No response.

I walked farther into the entry and looked around. Finally I saw a few people in the back. "Hello! I need help!"

A person, (I was too distraught to register their gender), slowly walked up and said, "Yes?"

"My father needs help, he'll probably need a wheelchair. He's in the car."

"Okay," they said.

I ran back to the car quickly, praying my father was still conscious and hadn't given up on me. I hated leaving him alone for what felt like ten minutes.

Two guys came out and helped my dad into a wheelchair. I couldn't look at him knowing he was in so much pain from being jostled around. They took him back to an examination room and a nurse said I could sit in the waiting room. I read a magazine and wanted to be taken away by the words so badly I surprisingly processed what I read.

Watching my dad suffer while my mother was gone wasn't supposed to happen. How did this end up as my life? My dad never asked that question. He told me he didn't have any regrets. How could he not ask how or why he was dying at 53 years old? A recently retired man with a healthy lifestyle? A man with so much more of life ahead of him? Why this misfortune?

They gave my father a shot of strong pain medicine in his back, gave him a prescription, and told him he could go home if he wanted. He said he could feel the comfort from the shot gradually fading away.

I picked up his prescription and took him home. Thank God we had decided to hook up the buzzer just in case. What if we hadn't hooked up the buzzer *and* tested it? He couldn't have gotten up, could he? He may have made it to the intercom, but would I have heard his weak voice through my deep sleep? Yes, I would have. The lighthouse in a dark sea. I would have.

Candle

I found my father's candle, which I had lit at our first ceremony. Though I probably wouldn't be able to light a candle at City Hall, I would still bring it in my bag with me to the hotel. Now I needed a candle that would represent my mother, too.

I went to craft stores trying to find something. I wasn't satisfied with any of the choices. I had given up for a while, and it wasn't until meeting at the funeral home to make the arrangements and decisions for my mother's funeral that I found my candle.

Since I was my mother's only child, and because of Tom's laid-back personality, I knew he would let me make most of the funeral decisions that Mom hadn't already made.

Tom sat across the table from me, and my three aunts and Donna were there to support us. I let Tom choose most of the personalized scripture readings and some songs and the thank you card message. We agreed on most things including the image of the lop-eared bunny in her casket. The funeral director had told us that we could pick an image that would go on her memory candle.

"I didn't know we got a candle," I said, looking at the image book.

Tom looked through it, too.

"You can pick," I told him.

He seemed indecisive and hesitated. I could tell he wanted to pick something meaningful. He was more caring than what you would assume most men to be.

Then finally he saw it.

"This one is her," he said, knowing my mother would have chosen it for herself.

"That's perfect," I said.

It had an angel, a bunny, and a lighthouse. Mom loved angels and her favorite animal was the rabbit. Her entire family knew her by her nickname, "Bunny."

The lighthouse was a symbol my mother had adopted over the years. Her house was decorated with nautical décor and an extreme amount of lighthouse memorabilia. The lighthouse had always been the love symbol for her love with my father. It's one of the main symbols in "Pete's Dragon," one of the first films my parents saw together in the theatre. The theme song is "Candle on the Water."

After Mom passed away I read the lyrics. It was like she was speaking to me with the words. The lyrics are:

"Candle On The Water"

I'll be your candle on the water
My love for you will always burn
I know you're lost and drifting
But the clouds are lifting
Don't give up you'll have somewhere to turn

I'll be your candle on the water
'Till ev'ry wave is warm and bright
My soul is there beside you
Let this candle guide you
Soon you'll see a golden stream of light

A cold and friendless tide has found you
Don't let the stormy darkness pull you down
I'll paint a ray of hope around you
Circling in the air
Lighted by a prayer

I'll be your candle on the water
This flame inside of me will grow
Keep holding on you'll make it
Here's my hand so take it
Look for me reaching out to show
As sure as rivers flow
I'll never let you go
I'll never let you go
I'll never let you go…

When we were making photo boards for Mom's funeral, Tom came across a video of Mom speaking at a candle lighting "luminar" ceremony. It was the walk for cancer at Tom's daughter's college in Washington called, "Relay for Life." As a survivor Mom had been invited to speak.

Tom called us all around to listen to the video. Aunt Quiet, Uncle Quiet, Aunt Giggly, Donna, and I came in to the cluttered office room. The video was too dark to see her face. Maybe Tom just wanted to hear her voice again.

Mom got on stage to speak, though you couldn't see much besides a small light in the rain and darkness. It was April 2011.

"Thank you for welcoming me here. This is the first time that I have been at a relay and been part of it, and I tell you when I took that walk around with the survivors it was unbelievable. I still have some cancer now and so I'm kind of still recovering and trying to get my strength back, and that really gave me the strength. And to see all of you on the sidelines clapping and just being there for all the other survivors and showing that love was unbelievable, so thank you all for doing that.

"I am a breast cancer survivor. I was diagnosed in 2003 and it has come back now. And actually it's gone out of my bones now, but I have it in my lungs and that's what I'm being treated for. I also had a little bit in my brain and so I had radiation. And a while after radiation I started to lose some of the hair in kind of a halo around my head. And I thought well, there's a lot of brain tissue in there, so I asked the doctor, I said, 'Well what kind of effects do you think that has?' And she said, 'Don't worry about it.' But you know I'm gonna be 60 this year and any thought of losing any of those brain cells any faster is not comforting!"

She chuckled, nervous, but strong.

"My story starts in 2001. My late husband, Mike, was diagnosed with pancreatic cancer, so I was a caregiver to begin with. But through his strength our faith, our hope, our love, and our trust in God, made the six-and-a-half months that he lived something to help me to go on later, which I didn't know that I would need, but it was a beautiful example to me of how to deal with it. So seven months after he died I came down with the breast cancer, but I knew the breast cancer was survivable, unlike the pancreatic cancer at that time. So it didn't bother me so much because I knew what had gone on. My biggest thing at the time was I didn't have anyone to be there for me like I was able to be there for my husband. But through faith and by the grace of God he brought Tom into my life and he's been my help and my support through all of this, and it's just been wonderful.

"I looked at this as I was trying to decide what to say tonight: 'God provided what I didn't know I needed or even wanted.' I wasn't thinking about another husband. And then when Tom came into my life, he provided what I didn't know I needed or wanted. He gave me three stepdaughters, a son-in-law and grandkids. But my grandkids provided what I know we all want, more time and love.

"And with my cancer I found a lot of trust and faith in god. I spent a lot of years trying to do things my way- didn't work out real well. And once I started trusting God, he had his plan of how to take care of things.

"Cancer does slow you down and it is one day at a time, but it lets you live in the present. I was one that was always planning far out into the future. Now you live in the present you make the most of every day and you show the people around you how much you love them all the time.

"I thought this is an opportunity for me to reach out and tell you, when I meet other people we just go, what if people didn't have faith? How can they get through this? Because it is important to know there is someone out there who loves you so much and wants to take care of you.

"I just wanna say again how much I appreciate you being here and in the rain and what you have meant to my life. God bless all you survivors out there and caregivers and family. Thank you".

After the crowd applauded, the host thanked my mother and then said:

"Tonight we honor and or remember those for whom we have lit candles. This light represents the love we have for you. It burns for others to see, but it burns brightest in our hearts. Now let's pause for a few moments to honor our loved ones."

Video

We decided to use the videographer who filmed our last ceremony, but a week before the ceremony she broke her ankle and had to cancel. Forced to go back to Craigslist last minute, I tried not to get anxious.

I had wanted to make a video of Mom talking to the baby before she died so at least he would have a message from his Grandma if he never got to meet her. It was still too early to tell if it was a girl or a boy, so Donna and I just called the baby in my belly, "Boo Bear." I think it came about from jokes Donna made about Papa Johns that went to Poopoo Johns, to Booboo John, to Boo Bear.

A month after I found out I was pregnant was when we found out Mom probably wouldn't live to see the baby. I went to the store and brought in a bag to Mom's room.

"Mom, remember when your friend got cancer and her goal was to see her daughter graduate from high school? You told her to count the days and put that number of stones in a jar and take one out every day to count down the days she had to hold on. Well I bought some for you."

I pulled out a glass vase that said "Celebrate Life" on it and pink-colored glass stones with variations of hearts, sparkly ones, and clear diamonds. The colors looked like the breast cancer color theme.

I counted out the days until I was due. It seemed like so many.

"It's beautiful," she said. "You can take one out for me for today."

I stared at the stones after she died. I counted them. 180 left. For a moment I was mad at them. Mad at the number of days that were inevitable. Mad at the time which couldn't be changed, outrun, or beaten. Mad at the unfairness and the what-ifs. Mad at those 180 days of an entire lifetime.

But then I thought about it a different way. It was 180 days she didn't have to feel pain.

I had been waiting for the right time to take the video of Mom for the baby when she had more energy and there were fewer visitors.

But she just kept getting weaker and more people came over.

Finally one morning I came in and she was just resting.

"We need to do that video soon, Mom, maybe today. Let me know when would be a good time."

"We can do it now," she said.

I had hoped for more energy and a longer video, but it was priceless and I was lucky to get it two days before she died.

She looked at the camera, lying back in her bed, and slowly spoke:

"Hi Baby. I'm so sorry I'm not going to be able to meet you. I guess Kelly and Donna call you Boo Bear right now. And I gave you a little bear that has a little blanket and I hope you enjoy that. And know that I would have loved you very much and I wish I could have been there to hold you and to rock you and to show your moms how much I really love you. I hope you grow up in a loving household. And I just want you to know how much I would have wanted you to be there with me. And I would have been able to give you all kinds of birthday cards and presents. And…I love your mothers so much. So you take care and I'll see you in Heaven. Bubye."

I turned off the camera and wiped a few tears with my sleeve I hadn't been able to before, having been trying to hold the camera steady.

Mom told me to look under the bed. There was a box.

"Open it," she said.

It was a cross-stitched baby bib.

"I did it a month ago. Luckily I finished before my fingers became too weak," she said.

The bib was quilted and white with ties. Since she didn't know the baby's gender it was more generic in theme with a purple dragon, a yellow castle, and a pink bear.

"I don't think I can let the baby wear it, it's too special. Maybe I'll frame it," I said holding back tears. "I had no idea you did this. It means so much. Thanks, Mom."

She smiled and rested her eyes.

Invitations

When I told Mom I was pregnant she gave me two diaries she wrote; one when she was pregnant with me and one when I was a baby. I didn't want to spend the time looking at them when she was still alive; I wanted that time with her. I tried to read a bit when she napped, but I didn't get very far.

One night, months later, I came across her diaries, which I had stored in our safe. They were priceless to me, of course, like my father's notes to me.

I paged through the one when she was pregnant. Photos and cards were pasted onto the notebook pages like a scrapbook. Mom saved notes and newspaper articles. She had written down what everyone had bought her for her shower. Then I noticed she had saved the invitation for the shower her sisters had given her.

It was December 1980, on a Sunday at 2 p.m. in Fridley, MN. The shower was given by her three sisters, the same ones who were throwing me a shower in a couple weeks. My shower was on a Sunday at 2 p.m., and just happened to be Fridley, also, though I lived 45 minutes from there. Uncle Pete had just moved to that area and had a party room in his apartment building. We chose it because it was free and somewhat of a central location.

The similarities of the showers were a coincidence. My aunts hadn't recalled the details of my mother's shower 33 years ago.

I touched the pages of my mother's diary, which was in a three-ring binder and must have been rewritten at some point neatly on notebook paper like she had planned to give it to me.

When you start having your own children you begin to sincerely appreciate what your mother went through just to have you and take care of you. It's at that time when you can thank her wholeheartedly and tell her how much you appreciate her raising you. It was this time that my mother would miss just by seven months. And she would also miss my legal marriage by fewer than three months.

I hugged the diary before putting it away in the fireproof safe.

At my mother's funeral there was a lady there who looked so familiar but I just couldn't place her. A cousin maybe, a work colleague? She was there by herself and didn't seem to know anyone else. She looked around and then seemed ready to leave. Our eyes met. I could have just let her leave but I wanted to know who she was.

I approached her.

"Hi. You look so familiar. Do I know you?" I asked.

"I was your parents' mail lady," she said.

It must be strange delivering mail to the dead. But the dead get mail all the time. From those who didn't know they were dead, to debt collectors, advertisements, scams, etc. My mother still got mail. But she would not get a wedding invitation this time. No one would.

The organizer for the legal marriage ceremony emailed us telling us we could now invite 25 guests instead of just 10. The invitations to our early morning ceremony wouldn't have fancy stationery or envelopes. They wouldn't have hand-made paper cranes or stickers. They wouldn't have colors or a stylish font. They wouldn't need return labels or stamps.

It would be the most modern and convenient of technologies this time: a Facebook message or a text message.

It was too early in the morning for Donna's older family members. I invited Tom, my favorite cousin, one aunt, and our close friends. It was a week night, so many people had to get up for work the next day.

Donna and I invited our current realtor, Lynn. Lynn was down to earth, hip, and funny. She was the first realtor Donna and I both adored and we worked well with her. We were looking for a house big enough for a family of four, and in time for the baby.

From what was translated to me from a handful of phone conversations, it seemed as if Donna's father was confused and not welcoming my pregnancy; whether it was his biological grandchild or not didn't seem to matter to him. I could tell that hurt Donna more than me.

And I could only hope that when he held the grandchild my mother would never see, that he would love it as his own.

Cake

I could cross cake off my list. Those getting married at City Hall would get free cake and their picture taken in front of a six-foot cake.

<u>December 2011</u>
Mom and I hadn't baked or decorated cakes or cupcakes together since before Dad died, but ten years later Mom asked me to help her with cupcakes. This time it was a funeral theme. It was her father's.

After going into an assisted living home, Grandpa started going downhill. I told myself I would speak at the funeral. I tried to stay strong, seeing another man in my family who was dying. I expected to be used to it by now, but it was harder.

"Grandpa, I just wanted to tell you I love you and that you were the best grandpa," I said trying to hold back tears.

"I don't think I did much," he said.

"You loved us. That's the most important thing."

"I love you, sweetheart," he said, returning my hug the best he could. Even though he had a lot of pain in his back he still made jokes and told us he loved us. He also told his care nurses that he loved them.

Like my other two grandparents and both of my parents, my grandpa had cancer, yet he didn't die from his slow moving leukemia, ironically. Back pain and medication that takes away your appetite don't give an 82-year-old man many more tolerable months of living.

The most recent children's book I illustrated I dedicated to him. It was called <u>Real Norwegians Eat Lutefisk</u>. He was the reason I knew my relatives in Norway and other states, and the reason Mom dragged me across the country for all their funerals.

Mom was exhausted from the funeral plans, cleaning out Grandpa's things, dealing with her younger siblings, and most of all her radiation and chemo treatments. I drove over to her house to frost the cupcakes. They were lemon, Grandpa's favorite. Tom came in and out of the house, working in the garage. My feelings started spilling out of me as I frosted the cupcakes.

"Mom, I want to spend more quality time with you."

"We just went to the mall not that long ago," she said right away.

"You are so busy with your schedule. I only want to make time to see you."

She became immediately defensive. "I've never said you couldn't come over here. Have I ever said you couldn't come over?"

"We've been busy with things," Tom said.

"You've been busy with your own life," Mom said to me, ignoring Tom.

"I know, Mom, but when I have a full-time job and a baby I'm going to be a lot busier, so I'm trying to make time now, before it's too late," I said, fighting back tears.

"It's like that song about the cat in the cradle," Tom said. I wanted to tell him to shut up or that I just wanted to have this conversation with my mother, but I was too frustrated to speak to him.

"I don't know what more you want from me. I'm having a hard time dealing with my parents' things and doctor appointments," Mom said.

I could tell she was getting physically tired from standing at the counter. Tom went outside. I sighed, relieved.

"I just want to spend time with you without distractions," I said.

"Where is that place? Tell me where that place is."

"Mom, it's really hard to talk to you. I'm trying to tell you what I need and it's hard for me. This doesn't have to be so difficult. You are making this sound impossible."

She sat down at the counter and put her head down and held it with her hands. She then looked up at me with a strong face, keeping her defensive vibe. Her red hair color had faded since she stopped dying it. She was nearly bald now.

I wiped away tears and struggled with words. "I don't consider it quality time when we meet up with other people. I want there to be time for just you and me."

"Just tell me what you want. What do you want?"

"I want you to stop raising your voice at me right now," I said bluntly.

She finally took a moment to hear what I was saying.

"I'm willing to make more effort to find time to spend with you. I want a better relationship with you. I don't feel your love anymore, Mom. I want a hug now and then. That's all I want."

She put her head back against the chair and closed her eyes, resting her brain from stress.

I walked over to her and bent down and hugged her. She hugged me back.

We went into her bedroom so she could rest. I lay down next to her on the bed.

"I'm sorry you lost your dad and your grandpa," she said.

"I'm sorry you lost the love of your life and your dad," I said.

"I think I closed off since your dad died. I haven't been very loving towards you. I haven't let myself be emotional. I would just fall apart from all this if I let myself feel," she said. The first tear I saw on my mother's face in years slowly fell down her cheek and onto the pillow.

It all made sense to me now. She had put up a shield around her to keep the hurt from coming in, but it also kept the love from coming out.

"I'm sorry," she said.

"It's okay."

I held her hand as she closed her eyes and rested. I felt a sense of peace. Something in my mother had changed. She finally understood what I needed from her. All I needed was her love and presence.

"Why don't you get us two cupcakes?" Mom asked. "And don't let Tom see, 'cause I don't let him eat in bed." I could tell without looking that she was smiling with her eyes closed.

*

I wouldn't make a cake for mom's funeral. The cake baker was dead. There wouldn't be her homemade frosting in the freezer anymore. Anything I wanted to eat she used to make for me I would have to make myself now. No homemade apple pie with extra cinnamon at Thanksgiving. No decorated cakes for birthdays, recitals, over the hills, funerals. Those would disappear with her. So much more of my life was gone than I could realize. The only things left were memories and the smell of frosting.

Flowers

Growing up, the one cake-decorating technique my mother used that I could never quite master was flower-making. It not only took a certain tip to create the curved petals, but you had to hold the bag of frosting at an angle and squeeze the right amount. You also had to make sure to let go smoothly while turning the metal base the flower sits on.

Before putting it in the fridge to harden, you add my favorite part which were the leaves. The leaves were the most fun because of the special tip. The tip had a dip in the center to create the middle vein of the leaf. If you lifted it up and down once or twice while applying the frosting, it put a curl in the leaf to make it look more real. You also had to pull gently at the end when you stopped squeezing the frosting bag to make sure the leaf was left with a nice, thin, natural point.

I would watch as my mother would hold the metal base with waxed paper on it and create so seamlessly a light purple flower bud with perfect petals and mint-colored leaves to embrace it.

Mom also had a grass tip that created blades of grass. I wasn't patient enough to slowly pull the tip away from the output of frosting at the end, so my blades of grass never looked as nice as my mother's steady hand creations.

Before Mom's funeral, my friend Holly offered to supply the flowers and create a casket topper for my mother. Mom loved calla lilies and told me before she died she would like those. Tom and I decided on purple and white.

The perfect arrangement consisted of pure white roses huddled together with lime green leafy plants filling in spaces between white orchids with pink centers and smaller white orchids clustered on stems. The white calla lilies emerged out and upwards with long stems, towering above the rest. Their centers were a dark magenta with a yellow stamen. Three orange fake butterflies were attached to the long stems. Four purple ribbons reached out from beneath the spread that said Grandma, Mother, Sister, Wife.

I associated the smell of lilies with death, but thankfully the aroma from the calla lilies wasn't like other lilies.

148

Aunt Giggly picked out a giant rosary made of lilac-colored roses to hang inside the casket, representing Mom's strong faith and dedication to prayer.

After the funeral all the flower arrangements in pots and vases sat in Tom's house. I grabbed some to take home and some to give away. Weeks later when I stopped back at Tom's place, the ones I hadn't taken still sat there rotting like corpses.

Donna and I definitely wanted flowers in our hair for the ceremony, but we couldn't decide if we wanted bouquets to carry this time. We didn't know if our wedding party or witnesses were allowed to stand up with us and the Mayor, so there might not be a place to put our flowers while we exchanged rings. Many of the details were still unknown to us while we were planning. The anal planner in me didn't sit well with that.

Rings

When Mom was dying she asked me to grab the boxes of her jewelry she kept in the closet.

"Pick out which ones you like," she said to me. "I bought these ones in Italy. This one was from Greece," she said pointing.

I could tell by her eyes and voice that she was tired. She didn't have much energy to pick up her arms to move the small jewelry boxes.

"These I bought in Arizona and these I got with your dad when we went to Florida."

"I remember," I said.

I didn't like expensive jewelry but I wanted to hold on to as many pieces of her as I could.

"Did you still want me to keep your ring with Tom and put on your ring with Dad?"

"Yes, but I don't know if it will fit."

We tried. It didn't fit over her swollen fingers.

"Maybe you can put it on your necklace chain?"

"That's a good idea."

I grabbed the necklace she picked out to be buried in. It was a gold anchor with Christ on it like the anchor was his cross. I strung the ring on it.

"That works," she said.

How would I tell Tom that Mom wanted me to keep her black coral ring they bought together? I didn't know what I would do with it, but she kept insisting I keep it because it was a piece of art, so I did.

Tom was acting strange about who got what piece of jewelry and he wanted to tell the story behind it and know who would be wearing it. This behavior made my three aunts uncomfortable about the jewelry Mom gave them.

"What jewelry did you guys get of hers?" he asked my aunts the day after Mom died.

They showed him their bracelets and necklaces. He proceeded to tell them how much they cost so in his mind they could appreciate them more, but it only came across as awkward and rude.

I showed Tom the black coral ring that was similar to his.

"Mom told me to keep this because it is a piece of art," I said.

"Oh. Okay," was all he said.

I had wished I knew what he was thinking, but then I decided I didn't want to know in case my keeping the wedding ring hurt his feelings.

My mother's fingers were slightly smaller than mine, so, just like her shoes, I didn't fit into any of her rings.

Donna and I bought one last pair of rings for our legal marriage because our cheap ones had weathered and we wanted ones that matched better. White gold bands with small diamonds on one side that lay flat. Simple, affordable, and practical.

Music

The Twin Cities Gay Men's Chorus was going to sing at City Hall and some other local artists before the first couple, who happened to be women, would get married. We didn't know what kind of music they would play, if any, while we walked down the steps, so I could cross music off my list, also.

When I was working full-time as an illustrator for a company, I had told one of my Christian coworkers I was gay, only because she asked if I had a boyfriend. She didn't take it well and she felt I should tell our boss since we were a small company working closely together like a family. I didn't care if my boss knew, and though I didn't think he needed to know, I told him just so she would stop asking me to tell him. He handled it like an idiot, not knowing what to say, but still making a long speech that had nothing to do with anything. Overall he didn't care, but the experience influenced me enough to write a song called, "The Way That I Love."

A few days before my mother died I played her the CD of songs I wrote and recorded that I had never shared with her before. I had been too shy about them since I wasn't professional and didn't always sing on key.

Once I performed one song for my mom and she said, "You should take voice lessons." After my lessons I had a recital which she attended. She told me, "It was good, but I can't say much about the song you played because I don't know it. But I'm impressed you could get up in front of lots of people and play."

When I played the CD for her, she rested and listened in between phone calls, the news, visitors. I noticed her attention span fading and her tiredness as the day was ending, so I picked one last song for her to listen to. It was "The Way That I Love."

The way that I love

You can lie in your made-up bed
Never caring what's in my head
No one can tell me how to use my heart.

I've been this way from the start

Who are you to say what's wrong or right
When there's infinite gray between black and white
If our eyes can see only 40 shades
What's the value when our heart decays?

When judgment goes away
We'll be left with the wise
Those that need not walk in my skin
But have changed their eyes.
I believe that God's on both our sides
Even when it burns after it collides

Let me show you the way that I love
It's not so different from the stars above
Goes on forever just like the sea
Below the earth the roots meet tree to tree.
Above the surface they are blind
Assuming love was too hard to find
So the secret is kept within
And assumes its empty place in the man of tin.

The way that I love may be different from yours
Tell me you wouldn't open a window in a room with no doors.

This is the way that I love
Goes on forever like the stars above

It's just one space but it's all around
Like a smallest echo is still a sound

May not matter when we're gone
But I know I did nothing wrong
But loved my way

Like there was only today.

Let me show you the way that I love
It's not so different you will see
Just remember that it comes from me.

One night, not long after Mom died, when I was pregnant and emotional, Donna and I had an argument. I left the house and drove to the neighborhood of the house we were considering buying and parked the car. In tears, I sat feeling more alone than I ever had in my life. Both of my parents were dead, Donna and I had a fight, Todd was at his dad's, and I couldn't see or hold the baby inside me yet.

Usually when I missed my dad I would turn on the oldies station on the radio and tell myself that my dad was the DJ. I'd hear songs he and I used to dance to. Tonight I turned the radio to the oldies station, looking at the dark graphite purple clouds, I asked out loud for both of my parents to give me a song, the next song on the radio. I wanted a message from them, something to cheer me up, remind me that life was worth living even when the ones I loved were dead.

The next song began. I'd never heard it before. The title was: "You Ain't Seen Nothin' Yet." I smiled as tears ran down my cheeks. Those were the best words from Heaven I could hear. But did that mean life would get worse or better? Maybe I hadn't seen the worst of my misery yet. But of course I knew better. I would see my baby and Donna and I would be legally recognized, and I would see my parents and the wonders of Heaven someday. Wonderful things were awaiting me.

<u>May 10, 2013</u>

The afternoon after mom died, my aunts were still over at Tom's house, as it was now Tom's house, no longer my parent's place, no longer Mom's place, and no longer Momtom's.

"Grandma's been trying to call me. She wants to know if she can come see your mom," Aunt Giggly said to me. "I made the mistake telling her I'm here and now she knows we are all here. I didn't want to tell her about your mom yet.

Also, I should tell you, before your mother died, she decided she didn't want us taking your grandma to the funeral. She would be too upset and then it would be harder for everyone to deal with it and the focus would be taken off your mom and on Grandma. We agreed with your mom."

I didn't agree, but I didn't know what to say. Mom had just died and we had to go make the funeral arrangements.

"Okay," I said.

May 11, 2013

"I don't understand why I can't go to my own daughter's funeral," Grandma said to me over the phone.

"I'm sorry, Grandma. I'll see what I can do and I'll see you tomorrow, okay?"

"Okay. I love you, honey."

"Love you, too."

That night I thought about it and didn't think it would be bad for Grandma and might actually be good for her. Seeing relatives, getting out, attention and closure. It was her daughter. She should go. Somehow I could make that happen. Mom didn't think Grandma could handle it, but I thought she could.

May 12, 2013. Mother's Day.

Ironically, only two days after my mother died it was Mother's Day. Donna and I went to visit my grandmother, the only one I had left.

I was not technically a mother yet, and it was too early to feel like one when I hadn't felt the kicks inside.

We met my aunts outside Grandma's door.

"I was thinking," I said, holding Donna's hand tightly, "Grandma should be able to come to the funeral."

Donna and I had talked the night before. She had told me to be strong and stand up to my aunts if it's what I believed, but I knew them well. They were also trying to honor my mother's wishes.

"I know, but it's not going to happen. It's not just about the money we would have to pay to have someone move her and take her there; it's also the legal responsibility. She had started to accept that she wouldn't be going and then your Great Aunt Pam called this morning and offered to take her and it started all over again," Aunt Giggly said.

"I think seeing people would be good for her," I told my aunt.

"Yes, but she had a breakdown the other night and the nurse had to give her meds. She has finally calmed down and accepted she won't be going."

"Uncle Pete wanted to take her, too, but we convinced him not to. We will all back each other up on this," Aunt Quiet said.

I let out the breath inside of me, but held the disappointment as I tried to accept that Grandma wouldn't be there.

I walked into her room and gave her a hug.

Her room was the typical one bedroom nursing home room, except was in the Memory Care Unit. The room contained a bed, similar to the hospital type beds my parents died in, a chair, a desk, and a dresser. Her desk sat between the attached closet and bathroom. The walls and dresser were full of photos of my Grandpa, their seven children, twelve grandchildren, and fourteen great-grandchildren.

"Happy Mother's Day, Grandma," I said.

"They won't let me go," she said and paused, "but cousin Allan is going to film it and I can watch it later."

Donna hugged her.

"Love you, Grandma," Donna said.

"Love you, too, honey," she said.

I felt bad for her, but better that she was accepting it. If it was me I don't think I could ever accept not being able to attend my own child's funeral.

"She was my first baby," Grandma said.

I looked at her eyes to tell me her tone because I couldn't tell by her voice. She was calm. She was going to be okay. I smiled and hugged her again and thought about my first baby, still inside of me.

May 13, 2013

The day after Mother's Day, the Minnesota Senate voted 37 to 30 in favor of the freedom to marry for same-sex couples, the final vote needed to send the bill to Governor Dayton to sign into law.

156

Last election day, Donna had to work so she asked me to take her parents to go vote. I felt awkward as my minimal Vietnamese was still more than they knew in English and I couldn't translate to help them vote if I needed to.

"Obama good guy?" her father asked me in his broken English which I had never heard anything besides 'Thank You' before.

"Obama good guy," I said.

Her mother giggled.

The ballot that year for Minnesota contained the vote to amend the constitution to limit marriage to only between a man and a woman. A vote 'Yes' would support that and stop Donna and I from getting legally married. A vote 'No' would open up possibilities for same sex marriage becoming legal.

I thought about telling her parents to check 'No.' They didn't know what it said. Donna's parents were traditional Vietnamese, so if I had translated it her father would probably not agree with picking 'No.' Her mom liked to please people so she would probably see my smile and pick it. But I couldn't translate it.

I looked down at their ballots after they checked 'Obama.' They wanted me to make sure they had done it correctly. I looked around in the voting room. I could easily check the 'No' box for both of them.

I hesitated, but then decided I didn't want to be dishonest and swing their vote, even for Donna's and my benefit. Also wasn't it illegal to vote for someone else? I put their ballots in the box. As we walked out I kept thinking I should have just checked the 'No' box.

Later I found out not checking any box ended up still counting as a 'No' vote and we won! That victory felt so sweet, knowing we were on our way to legal marriage.

May 14, 2013

Governor Mark Dayton signed the freedom to marry into law, making Minnesota the 12th state where same-sex marriage was legal, the day of my mother's wake.

May 15, 2013

Yesterday had been a celebration of a victory followed by a tragedy, yet still a celebration- a celebration of my mother's life.

The family said the rosary before the funeral service. My hands moved over the silver beads like my mother's had done several times a day. I looked over to Aunt Quiet, holding one of my mother's many rosaries Tom gave to everyone who wanted one. She caught my eye and showed me her wrist. It was a tattoo of a pink breast cancer ribbon with my mother's nickname, Bunny, and date she died: May 10, 2013.

Everyone shows their love and loss in different ways. I smiled, admiring her tattoo, the permanent symbol of eternal love and dedication to my mother from her sister.

"We are gathered here today to celebrate the life of Brenda Frankenberg," the priest said when the funeral started.

When everyone is expecting you to be sad and fall apart, that's the moment when I hold it together.

I was ready to give the eulogy. In my knee-length dress, black with pink Hawaiian flowers on it, I approached the podium. My belly of three months protruded just enough from the form-fitting dress and my small waist to tell there was something there.

"When I try to search for answers and reasons," I said. "I find one line in particular which comforts me, said by Virginia Woolf's character in 'The Hours.' She said, 'Someone has to die in order that the rest of us should value life more.'"

I paused and read more about my mother's life, staying steady and no tears.

"When she met my father, Mike, at a bowling alley, she knew he was the one."

I looked up at Donna.

"I asked Mom how she wanted to be remembered. She said 'As someone who was generous and kind and loving. She loved God and loved her neighbor.'"

I looked at Tom sitting in the pew, the union that was once Momtom, now just Tom, and tried to swallow down tears.

"My mother wanted a baby girl, and when I came one month early and was a handful, she knew she only wanted one. She had many step-children and step-grandchildren whom she enjoyed and was looking forward to my baby due this

158

October," I said, holding my belly, thinking of the irony of becoming a mother when I was losing mine.

"In her last days she embraced the philosophy my father had when he was dying, which was, 'I look forward to every day. When I wake up I will either be here with my family, or with God in Heaven'…And now she is."

Two and a half months later.

It was finally time to get legally married. I was ready, I was seven months pregnant, and I accepted my mother wouldn't be there.

A few weeks before the wedding there was a conference call with staff from the Mayor's office and the couples getting married. Questions came in one after the next. I tried to keep up with my checklist.

"Will others get to watch?"

"When can we pick up our marriage certificate?"

"When can our guests come?"

"How long can our vows be?"

Our vows were allowed to be one minute to a minute and a half. Who ever had to time their wedding vows?

July 31, 2013. Wedding time!

Donna and I arrived around 6 p.m. at Hotel Minneapolis within walking distance of City Hall. Since doors didn't open until 10:30, we had dinner before Holly and her assistant came to do our hair and makeup. Holly told me to allow them 4 hours for hair and makeup. I told her 3.

"I'm a little nervous," I told Donna, shaking from excitement, as I tried to relax and eat my salad. "I'm guessing Holly will be her quintessential 15 minutes late."

As Donna and I ordered dessert Holly texted.

"She'll meet us upstairs at our room in 10 minutes. She's parking."

"Great. Should we take the dessert to go?" Donna asked.

"It will probably melt, but oh well. We can eat it while they do our hair."

Holly's black curls hung just below her shoulders and revealed some subtle highlights in the light. Her makeup was always dramatic and made her look like a famous Bollywood actress. Our hotel room had one mirror across from the bed and one mirror by the small loveseat in the entry area. The mirror by the bed had better lighting because it was by the window, however the sun hid behind the city skyscrapers darkening the room. The couch was dark purple like Holly's darkest shade of purple eye shadow. It also matched her skirt.

We giggled about things from our childhood as she applied Donna's makeup and her assistant, Kayla, curled my hair.

"I think we should bump it up in the back," Holly said when she saw my hair.

"No, I don't want it to look too big and fake," I said.

"It won't. Trust me. Plus it will look great in photos."

"Okay. Just a little," I said, anxious.

"You ready for makeup?" Holly asked.

"Yes…wait, I should wash off my other makeup first, right?"

Holly gave me a puzzled look and leaned in and squinted.

"You're wearing makeup?"

She still squinted.

I frowned.

"Yes."

She leaned in closer.

"I'll wash it quick," I said.

Donna was in the bathroom and I came in.

"Apparently no one can tell I'm even wearing makeup. I guess she's just used to putting on so much," I said to Donna.

Donna smiled with her lips closed tightly to not say anything since I still had my frown.

After watching my caramel ice cream melt and slide off its sticky toffee cake cushion, my makeup was almost done. I looked in the mirror. Holly had put a lot of eyeliner on my eyes and I thought I looked like a doll. What could I say?

"I think it's too dramatic. Can you tone it down somehow?"

"Sure," she said.

"I think it looks good," Donna said.

"You just aren't used to seeing yourself like that," Kayla said, "But it really looks great!"

160

"It will look perfect in photos. Believe me," Holly said.

"No, it's still too much."

"Let me fix it. Come here," Holly said.

I started to get discouraged and worried I would look like a drag queen. Holly's makeup for our first wedding looked great. I told myself I just needed to get used to it. The fake eyelashes started to irritate my eyes.

"I think it's fine now," I said, looking in the mirror, hoping to believe it would look good in photos even if I didn't like it yet. "How about just gloss for lips, no color."

"Just a hint of color, my sister," Holly said.

I sighed, giving in.

10:30 p.m.- doors open.

Donna and I walked into City Hall and handed our tickets to a volunteer just beyond the entrance. Live music was playing loudly. We couldn't see the entertainment because it was blocked by walls and people. You could only get a viewing by going around to the sides to enter the atrium. We walked upstairs looking for a friend who had gotten tickets for the preshow. There were five floors and the balconies all overlooked the atrium.

Hot and dehydrated on the third floor, I asked Donna to get me some water. When Donna came back I was talking to an interviewer from MPR (Minnesota Public Radio).

Then a reporter from Channel 5 asked if we were getting married and if we could do an interview. Donna's shyness forced me to go first. Nervous, but enthused, I answered the reporter's questions.

"Just being legally wed and having children that have legally married parents is a huge deal for us," I said into the reporter's microphone.

The sound in the building was so loud we couldn't tell what was going on in the center on stage. After the interview we found one of our friends and she told us the Twin Cities Gay Men's Chorus was done and the Mayor was saying a few words.

11:45 p.m.- Mayor R.T. Rybak introduced Cathy ten Broeke and Margaret Miles, the first lesbian couple to get married. He started their ceremony, but it

161

went too quickly, four minutes too quickly. He couldn't legally pronounce them married until midnight exactly.

The Mayor stalled on stage, talking about how they met, until the four minutes had passed. The anticipation grew louder like a packed concert hall waiting for its favorite rockstar to return to the stage.

August 1, 2013. Our legal Wedding Day.

12:00 a.m.- "By the power now *finally* vested in me," the Mayor said, followed by roaring sounds so powerful and emotional you couldn't hear anything else, "by the laws of the people of Minnesota..." the Mayor, smiling, raised his voice to talk over the celebration noise. As he pronounced Cathy and Margaret legally married, their five-year-old son hugged them and they kissed.

Light flashed everywhere. More cheering than a parade echoed throughout the atrium and through the massive speakers. The 3rd floor of City Hall heated up. I stayed back from the crowd fanning myself with the paper schedule, hoping I wouldn't sweat off all my makeup and no one could see the sweat piling up on my belly through my white sheer dress.

Then a lady from the Star Tribune asked to take our photo. We were temporarily famous just for getting married.

After pronouncing the first gay male couple and an intermission, the Mayor was scheduled to perform weddings all the way until 6 a.m. We didn't know where we were in that line.

1:00 a.m.- Our guests were allowed to come in, but we had their tickets. We went outside to find them where I told them all to meet no later than 12:45. Outside there was a little breeze, but not much with all the venders and press waiting out front.

Donna stayed inside to catch guests as they walked in. I found a few at a time. I started getting nervous as time went by. What if it was our time to get married, how would we know?

After gathering just about everyone, we met our photographer and our videographer. We also finally got a volunteer assigned to us to help with the full wedding process.

Once the entire wedding party arrived, we were moved to a waiting room on the third floor before our ceremony time, which was still unknown to us. All our guests couldn't fit in one elevator and having only one volunteer and no signs in the area, some of our guests got lost. It took us a few trips before we all entered the waiting room.

Sweat lined the inside of my dress. It was still humid in City Hall's third floor with our 18 guests, our videographer, and our photographer, in a tiny conference room. I introduced each person since many of them hadn't met before.

Being seven months pregnant obviously wasn't helping with the heat. My sparkly white flip-flops matched my dress, but felt tight on my slightly swollen feet I shoved into them. After the introductions, I sat fanning myself.

The conference room contained tables, chairs, some sandwiches, plates, cups, and napkins. No one ate anything. Relieved to see our volunteer with a pitcher of water, I sighed. Our friend, Gabby, poured some for me, then Donna and Todd. Then a man entered the room.

"Can you fill out some information?" He asked and handed me some paperwork. "We will also need your driver's licenses. I'll bring a judge down to you, unless you want to meet me in the chamber, the council chamber," he said.

"What's the judge for?" I asked confused.

"The judge will marry you."

"But we were supposed to have the Mayor," I said, my eyes wide, starting to panic.

"Okay. We can get the Mayor. Sure," he said quickly.

"Ya, we were supposed to have him, for sure."

"Okay," he said.

"If that's possible," Donna said nicely.

"Absolutely," he said.

"We were told we have him," I said still unsure, ready to cry from exhaustion.

"We'll getcha," he said.

Donna looked at me.

"I don't have my license," she said.

I barely heard her, my focus was on the man.

"Take a breath, honey," Donna said.

"We didn't come this far to not get the Mayor," I said.

2:00 a.m.- The volunteer told us they ran out of the free wedding cake. I started worrying about how long this process was taking, having told our guests maybe an hour or two. I thought the photographer and videographer would charge me extra now that it was getting later and later into the morning.

"I don't have my license," Donna told one of the other volunteers holding paperwork.

"We just need it to see it. You can bring it tomorrow," he said.

"But we aren't going home right away," I said to Donna.

"Don't worry, honey, we'll figure it out," she said.

By this time my face felt like my make-up was running down it. My belly felt wet and hot under my dress, which felt tighter every minute. I pulled up the sides under my arms to adjust it. My sore and tired back met the back of the chair for support.

Donna poured me another glass of water. I drank it but worried I would have to pee again. Peeing with a long dress on with a big belly isn't a piece of cake, and they could call us at any minute. Our guests were becoming extremely tired, most having to be up in five hours for work the next day. Todd's head rested on the table.

"We can go now," the volunteer yelled when he peaked in.

All of the guests got up to follow.

City Hall was becoming less and less crowded as the night went on since people got married and left. News crews diminished.

Donna and I stood in line a floor above the infamous marriage steps. Our wedding party sat in the white chairs below. Originally we were told Todd and our witnesses had to wait down a floor with our other guests, but at the last minute our volunteer was informed they were supposed to be with us. We tried to get their attention below from the balcony, but there was another wedding going on and it was loud.

Our main volunteer, a tall man with white hair and glasses, was clearly agitated and ran to the elevator. The stairs in that area were just for the descending couples getting married.

"You ready?" another volunteer asked.

Donna and I turned around and luckily saw Todd coming towards us with our witnesses and our main volunteer who swore under his breath.

164

We turned and nodded. The Mayor, who had come up the steps during a short intermission, looked over our brief summary about us so he could choose a few personal words to add to his improvisation. Once he was back in his place in the center down the steps, they signaled us to come down.

2:14 a.m.-This was it. This was our 15 minutes of fame. This would be the legal binding of our hearts. The door for legal gay marriage opened and we stepped through it. Donna and I walked down the steps with Todd behind us and our witnesses: Alice and Lori. One white and one purple orchid lay pinned in Donna's hair, mine matching on the opposite side.

Donna's long black dress matched her black hair and the sparkles of her earrings reflected the silver glittered trim on her dress that lined her shoulders and criss-crossed her chest.

Mayor Rybak told us where to stand.

"Dearly beloved," he started. "We are gathered here tonight to celebrate the wedding of Kelly and Donna." His voice echoed in the open hall.

Cameras flashed and the crowd became quiet.

"Donna's mom told her," he started.

I knew he made a mistake. It was my mom. I didn't want to interrupt him, but I knew I had to.

"It was my mom," I said.

"Oh, sorry," he chuckled politely at his mistake, "Kelly's mom told her something pretty smart, she said, 'when you know, you know,' and she did. Because when Kelly and Donna met they knew immediately that they should be married, and that was three years ago. They are not only expecting to be married tonight, they are flat out expecting! They are expecting another child to join Todd, who is here with us today."

Applause.

"Would you like to share vows with each other?"

"Yes," I said. "Donna, in Vietnamese, Em là tất cả. It means…what does it mean…"

My mind went blank like it had the night I had forgotten what a dresser was. It was a simple phrase I knew and had written in my vows and yet I couldn't think.

Then my brain suddenly worked again. "It means you are my everything. And I will marry you every year for the rest of our lives."

"Beautiful," the Mayor said.

I handed Donna the microphone.

"Earlier I tried to look up lesbian vow sample, but I accidently typed in lesbian cows, so I got lots of YouTube videos that came up. But I didn't go there."

Mayor Rybak laughed out loud, but not as loud as our friend Gabby. Donna looked directly at me. I should have known she would take the dare.

"Anyway, just want to say thanks for accepting who I am and learning about my culture and language, definitely not easy language to learn. My culture really weird and strange and you put in a lot of efforts and show me how much you love me and love Todd. So starting a family together, there's nothing better in this world," Donna said and handed the microphone back to the Mayor.

"Want to exchange your rings? Todd, you're up," the Mayor said and gestured toward Todd. Todd handed him the rings from his pocket.

"You just did the most important thing. Good job," the Mayor said to Todd as Donna and I put our rings on each other.

"And now by the power *finally* vested in me, by the laws of the people of the state of Minnesota, I hereby legally declare that Kelly and Donna are legally married in the state of Minnesota. You may kiss the bride."

I leaned down to lessen the distance between Donna and I as our lips met.

"Pretty cool, huh?" the Mayor said to Todd who was smiling and clapping, now more awake.

The crowd erupted with cheers and camera flashes lit up the center of City Hall like a lightning storm.

Donna and I were finally legally married, and the ones I missed so deeply that day were still close in heart. No tears appeared, just love. And that's exactly what it was all about. Just love. And there's nothing wrong with that.

I stood proud and tall that day holding my belly, just like I did the day of Mom's funeral, giving the eulogy. As I held my belly I thought about what I was holding: the round home of new life covered in white satin. It wasn't just a beautiful coincidence. This was my door God opened when the door on life with my mother had closed. It was time to focus on the open door. I wasn't a

166

daughter anymore. I would be a mother. Life wasn't just taking away, life was giving. And... 'You ain't seen nothin' yet.'

References

Bachman-Turner Overdrive. "You Ain't Seen Nothin' Yet." You Ain't Seen Nothing Yet. 1974.

Cunningham, Michael. <u>The Hours</u>. Harper Collins. New York. 1998. Print.

<u>Desert Hearts</u>. Dir. Donna Deitch. Desert Heart Productions, 1985. Film.

Didion, Joan. <u>The Year of Magical Thinking</u>. Vintage International Edition. New York, Ny.2005. Print.

Dido. "See the Sun." Life For Rent. Artista Records. 2003.

Frankenberg, Kelly. <u>Cake Design</u>. Graphite & Digital. 2012. Image.

Frankenberg, Kelly. <u>Dress Designs</u>. Graphite & Ink. 2012. Image.

Frankenberg, Kelly. <u>Dress Designs 2</u>. Graphite. 2013. Image.

Frankenberg, Kelly. <u>Self Portrait</u>. Acrylic. 2002. Image.

Frankenberg, Kelly. "The Way That I Love." The Kid Inside. 2009.

Frankenberg, Kelly. <u>Unfinished</u>. Graphite. 2002. Image.

Frankenberg, Kelly. <u>Unfinished, Too</u>. Graphite. 2013. Image.

Frankenberg, Kelly. <u>Untitled Number 5</u>. Watercolor. 2003. Image.

Frankenberg, Kelly. <u>Wedding Party Sketch</u>. Ink. 2012. Image.

National Weather Service. <u>The May 6, 1965 Tornadoes</u>. Web. 5 Jan. 2012. <http://www.crh.noaa.gov/mpx/HistoricalEvents/1965May06/index.php>

Reddy, Helen. "Candle on the Water." By Al Kasha and Joel Hirschhorn. *Pete's Dragon*. 1977.

Kelly Frankenberg. <u>Self Portrait</u>. 2002.

Vita

Kelly Frankenberg is an artist, writer, and teacher and has a Master's of Fine Arts degree in Creative Writing from the University of New Orleans and a Bachelor's of Fine Arts degree in Illustration from the Minneapolis College of Art & Design. Her artwork has appeared on TV, in films, newspapers, magazines, books, the web, and on CDs, walls, mailboxes, and windows. She lives in Minnesota with her *legal* partner, their sons, and cats.

Visit:

www.diaryofagaypregnantbride.com

for events, updates, downloads, and more.

A portion of the proceeds of this book will be donated to LGBTQ charities and breast cancer research. For a complete list of charities visit the website.

For Kelly's new children's book series about her son, "Boo Bear," visit www.boobearsbookshelf.com